1″ = 1′ scale (2.5cm = 30.5cm) *General Store* by Joann McCracken. Acrylic clay heads, hands and feet. Wire armature bodies. *Photograph Courtesy of Chilton Book Company.*

# Petite Portraits

## Original Miniature Dolls by
## Contemporary American Doll Artists

by Carol-Lynn Rössel Waugh

Published by  **HOBBY HOUSE PRESS, INC.**
Cumberland, Maryland 21502

# Dedication

*For my young artists, Jenny-Lynn Waugh and Eric-Jon Rössel Waugh.*

*May 1982, Winthrop, Maine.*

Additional copies of this book may be purchased at $12.95
from
**Hobby House Press, Inc.**
900 Frederick Street
Cumberland, Maryland 21502
or from your favorite bookstore or dealer
Please add $1.25 postage

Printed in the United States of America
by Kirby Lithographic Company

ISBN: 0-87588-190-4

# Table of Contents

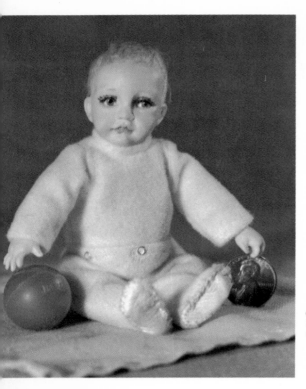

**Color Illustration 1.** 4in (10.2cm) *Gary* by Phyllis Wright. Porcelain head and lower limbs. Cloth body. © 1980.

**Color Illustration 2.** 8in (20.3cm) *La Danse* by Patricia Ryan Brooks. Hand-carved basswood multi-jointed with ball-joints. © 1981.

Color Illustration 3. 9in (22.9cm) *Firebird* by Carol Nordell. Composition with wire armature. 1981.

Color Illustration 4. 8in (20.3cm) *Elfreda* by Susanna Oroyan. Polyform with wire armature. Mohair wig. © 1981.

Color Illustration 5. 1'' = 1' scale (2.5cm = 30.5cm) *Mother Joy* and *Tiny Playmate* by Helen McCook. Porcelain bisque shoulder plates, lower limbs. Cloth bodies.

**Illustration I-1** EDGAR DEGAS (1834-1917): *Young Dancer of Fourteen Years* (Jeune Danseuse de Quatorze Ans). One-third life-size. Before 1881. Painted bronze statuette with white French tulle ballet skirt, satin ribbon in "hair." Costume bodice painted yellow. *Reproduced courtesy of the Metropolitan Museum of Art, New York, New York. Bequest of Mrs. H. O. Havemeyer, 1929. The H. O. Havemeyer Collection.*

**Illustration I-1A.** EDGAR DEGAS (1834-1917): *Young Dancer of Fourteen Years* (Jeune Danseuse de Quatorze Ans). Front view. This version of the statue is in the *Musee du Louvre, Jeu de Paume* in Paris, France. The bodice is painted a light yellow, and the skirt is fresher than the example of the statue in the Metropolitan Museum in New York. Just as an artist's statue may be done in editions, with each of the statues being considered an "original" by that artist, so may the work of a doll artist follow the same procedure.

# Introduction

This book is an introduction to a very demanding field of doll artistry, that of the miniature doll. Miniature dolls are dolls which are 9in (22.9cm) and under in size. Working in such a small scale is difficult. Problems of authenticity, articulation and execution are compounded when a sculpture verges on the microscopic. When it is tiny, any flaw is magnified and the risk of failure is great. When the designer is successful, however, his work has a gemlike quality. The following pages will profile the work of 52 doll artists who were active at this writing (1981).

The term DOLL ARTIST is little known and less understood, even to working artists, art historians and doll collectors, those who should be familiar with it. A doll artist, contrary to popular belief, does not paint portraits of dolls. He designs and executes original sculptures which are, incidentally, dolls.

The creation of a doll is the ultimate challenge for an artist. He must be conversant with many techniques and media to put together an entity which properly gives a semblance of life. Designing, carving, sculpting, modeling, mold making, painting, glazing, drawing, sewing, weaving, drafting, dyeing, a knowledge of portraiture, body language - anatomy and an insight into human behavior - - these are the subjects which a potential doll artist must master.

A doll artist is a sculptor working in a demanding field and in an exacting scale. Not only must his work be anatomically correct and pleasing to the eye, but, in many cases, it must be manipulable. Unlike the parts of a traditional fixated sculpture, the arms and legs of the art doll should be able to withstand the repeated repositioning and the not-so-gentle caresses of its often youthful owners, if the artist decides to articulate his work.

A doll artist usually considers himself a professional and aims for a high degree of quality and a strong aesthetic sense in his work. The keynote of his product is its vision, its uniqueness. A doll artist usually strives to design dolls which are different from any others, which express his inner vision of the world.

Artist dolls are, of necessity, done in small quantities. If an artist has any great artistic drives, he tires rapidly of doing the same thing over and over. Many doll artists only make one example of any doll they design. They enjoy the challenge of a new creation, a new concept, and rebel at the thought of doing it repeatedly. Instead, they go on to something else which appeals to them. These dolls are, obviously, termed "one-of-a-kind."

Some media demand one-of-a-kind dolls, even if the dolls may appear similar to each other. Wood, polyform, directly sculpted wax or fireable clay, modeled composition and needlesculpture all are examples of this.

Other media permit the production of editions of dolls. The question of editions is one which confuses many doll collectors who equate this doll making procedure with that of making reproductions. Let me try to explain by analogy.

A graphic artist, such as a lithographer or an etcher, will create an original drawing, either on a lithographic stone or on a metal surface. He will then reproduce this original drawing by printing it on paper through either the lithographic or the etching process. He, thereby, produces an EDITION of prints, each of which is considered an original, just as if it were a painting, and each is signed, numbered and dated. Each of these is one part of a multiple original. The prints made earliest in this procedure are considered, usually, the most desirable because they are closest to the artist's original conception, before the stone has begun to be worn down by the duplication process. Similarly, a sculptor may execute a statue in wax and cast, perhaps, six replicas of the wax in bronze. Each of these is considered an original.

A doll artist original edition works the same way. A doll artist working in porcelain, for example, may make a mold of her plastilina sculpture. From this she will perhaps cast a limited edition of 20 dolls. Each of these is considered an original. (Sometimes it is called an original edition.) It is signed and dated, just as is the print, and the earlier a doll is in an edition, the more desirable it is because, as each doll is made, the mold deteriorates slightly.

Artist dolls are almost always of limited editions because doll artists tire quickly of

1

Color Illustration 6. 1″ = 1′ scale (2.5cm = 30.5cm) *Family Portrait* by Carol Boyd. Porcelain bisque heads, lower limbs. Cloth bodies.

Color Illustration 7. 9in (22.9cm) *Porcina Rosebud* by Jean Heighton; 5¾in (14.7cm) *Voiletta* by Erin Libby. *Porcina Rosebud* is a ceramic all-bisque jointed pig baby. Dressed in white eyelet and lace. Inset glass eyes, felt tongue. 1981. *Violetta* has china painted porcelain bisque head, torso, limbs on padded wire armature. Cloth body. Mohair wig. Swivel head. © 1980.

**ABOVE LEFT: Color Illustration 8.** 7½in (19.1cm) *Mrs. C.* holding 2in (5.1cm) *doll* by Annie Shickell. China painted. Porcelain bisque shoulder plate and hands. Fabric body. Mohair wig. All-porcelain small doll with mohair wig.

**ABOVE RIGHT: Color Illustration 10.** 6in (15.2cm) *Henry* by Faith Wick. Porcelain bisque shoulder plate, lower limbs. Wire armatured cloth body. Molded hair.

**LOWER RIGHT: Color Illustration 9.** 5in (12.7cm) *Caucasian Infant* by Jeanne Singer. Porcelain head and limbs. Fabric body. 1980.

Illustration I-2. PATRICIA RYAN BROOKS: *La Danse.* 8in (20.3cm) tall. Polychromed basswood. Fully carved and articulated 13-piece ball-jointed body. All sockets lined with pigskin. Jointed at neck, shoulders, elbows, wrists, waist, hips and knees. Old French lace tutu. Yellow painted carved-on ballet costume. © 1981.

Illustration I-3. PATRICIA RYAN BROOKS: *La Danse.* Detail of Illustration I-2.

repeating themselves. This is why a doll artist doll, even if it is done in multiples, is a scarce commodity.

What does a collector buy when he purchases a doll artist original? He is buying a piece of articulated sculpture in miniature. He is buying one person's aesthetic interpretation of the human form. He is buying someone's heart and soul and vision - - something intimate and personal.

As with any other artistic category, there is a wide range of competence in the work of doll artists. The buyer should become fully familiar with the work of any artist who interests him. He should inspect it for quality and aesthetic sense. The above term is difficult to define because it is often purely subjective. Some artists appeal to one person and not to another. This does not mean, however, that the work of the latter is any less valid. Not everyone likes "Grandma Moses," Goya or Picasso, but each possessed a valid artistic vision.

Reproduction dolls are made by people who can best be described as doll artisans. In fact, the national association in America for reproduction-makers calls itself the DOLL ARTISAN GUILD. These people are specialists dedicated to the perpetuation of the techniques of recreating the dolls of the past. Some of these people are skilled craftsmen who produce beautiful products, but it must be remembered that they are reproducing someone else's sculptures.

A reproduction doll is one which is not the conception of the person making it. A reproduction doll need not be an antique replica, and it need not necessarily be made using purchased molds. It may be the reproduction of a contemporary doll artist's work by others, as is commonly done in the creation of convention doll souvenirs. In this case, the original doll is the sculpture the doll artist created for the doll, from which the reproduction molds were made. If someone other than the artist executes duplicates of the doll, then the duplicates are reproductions, not artist's editions.

The term "doll artist" is relatively new. It is specific and, perhaps, limiting. Gallery owners do not know how, or whether, to classify doll artist dolls when they are submitted for exhibition. They seem to be blinded by the dolls' color and by their preconceived notion of what a doll is and its traditional place in the art world, which is tenuous.

4

Sculpture is thought of as monochromatic and stationary by many people, although contemporary art history gives the lie to these notions. In fact, ancient art gives us numerous antecedents of contemporary doll sculpture. The Egyptians made statues of many media that were highly colored. Some of them were even clothed. Ancient Greek statues were not the pristine white they appear to be today. They were polychromed so that they could be seen from afar in the bright southern light. Some of these were, moreover, dressed in materials different from those of the bodies of the sculptures.

The 19th century produced perhaps the artistic grandfather of the contemporary doll artist. He never would have recognized the term, for he considered himself to be an artist in other media. He was a painter, a sculptor and a recorder of the human body in at times awkward, but truthful, poses. In 1880 to 1881, he exhibited the most famous artist doll of all time, *Jeune Danseuse de Quatorze Ans* (Young Dancer of Fourteen Years). His name was Edgar Degas.

Today this little girl is known through the several PAINTED AND DRESSED bronze casts of Degas' original sculpture. However, this one-third-life-size sculpture, which took six years to complete, was modeled in flesh-colored wax which was then painted. The dancer was sculpted nude and then dressed. Her linen bodice copied the lines of contemporary ballet clothing and was rendered in miniature, attached to the sculpture and then waxed. It was later painted. The skirt of frilly tulle was added and left in its natural state for contrast. Her wig of black human hair was obtained from a Parisian *maker of dolls and marionettes.* To this was added a hair ribbon that complemented the tutu.

When Degas' dancer was exhibited at the sixth salon of the Impressionists, spectators did not know what to do with it. They thought it was undignified, untraditional and awkward. It certainly was not the contemporary idea of sculpture. Today this doll is considered a masterpiece by many.

The work of two contemporary doll artists can be favorably compared with that of Degas.

Patricia Ryan Brooks' 8in (20.3cm) wooden figure, *La Danse* has many points in common with that of Degas. Both are of a young woman dancer in a yellow leotard with white tutu. The bodice of the garment of each doll is an integral part of the torso of the sculpture. The frilly white tutu provides contrast in color and texture. The hair of both figures is drawn back from the face. Each is carefully thought out as to purpose. But they convey contradictory emotions. Degas' little girl exemplifies repose, almost pensive solitude. The Brooks doll is full of action. Indeed, her ball-jointed body construction is such that she can be positioned innumerable ways. She is jointed at arms, head, waist, knees, elbows and wrists. Suspended from a flying metal arc, she can literally pirouette before one's eyes. The carving and engineering of the myriad of parts that comprise this sculpture is of exceptional quality. They helped its creator gain membership in NIADA, the National Institute of American Doll Artists.

Another NIADA artist, Carol Nordell, offers a completely different interpretation of a ballet dancer. Her *Firebird* is a stationary sculpture, as is Degas'. Like his work, it offers fascinating viewpoints as one walks around it. The dancer is designed to be seen from various angles, and one's perspective of it changes as he does so.

*Firebird* is modeled of composition in a very difficult, swooping pose. One can almost see the muscles and tendons in the dancer's body expand and contract as she moves. The flame-like colors of her costume highlight her action, and her preoccupied, almost sad expression adds a note of poignancy.

**Illustration I-4.** CAROL NORDELL: *Firebird.* 8in (20.3cm) standing height. Composition over wire armature. ©1981.

5

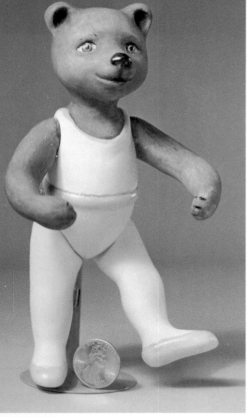

**ABOVE: Color Illustration 12.** 4½in (11.5cm) *Bear* by Patti Hale. Hand-carved jelutong wood. Jointed at head, arms and legs. 1980.

**ABOVE LEFT:** **Color Illustration 11.** 6in (15.2cm) *Bearishnikov* by Carol-Lynn Waugh. All-porcelain dancer bear. Five-piece construction. Jointed at arms and legs. Molded-on leotard and ballet slippers. © 1981.

**LEFT:** **Color Illustration 13.** 5in (12.7cm) *Medieval Lady* by Joann Marion Scott.

ABOVE: Color Illustration 14. *Nursery Rhyme Characters* by Jan and Lyn Gabrielson.

RIGHT: Color Illustration 15. *Dragonfly Lady,* Phantasmata series by Margaret Finch. Needlesculpted cloth over wire armature. © 1981.

There are those who will object to the term "sculptor" being used to describe the creators of art dolls. Some people look upon this work the same way the critics of the work of Degas did. Because they have no formal frame of reference, no convenient mental niche into which they can place this work, they refuse to acknowledge it as art at all, seeing only the "doll" aspect of it.

Most certainly art dolls are dolls, but they are also, at times, fine sculptures. Their creators have chosen a universally recognized form by which to express their ideas on the human condition. At times, the figures they choose for this task are not even human, but humanoid. An upright animal or half-animal, with human stance and dress, can often better express a concept than can a human figure, especially if this idea is a satiric one. This anthropomorphism has been practiced from before the time of Aesop. Some of the best "dolls" may actually be goats or bears or even ballerina frogs.

It will be some time before the art doll is accepted by the art establishment as a valid aesthetic statement. Education and exposure are necessary to accomplish this. The place of the art doll in the doll collectors' world is equally nebulous. Collectors are unsure of their value and pedigree. But, gradually, the doll artist doll is gaining in popularity as its quality and scarcity is appreciated.

With antique dolls' prices skyrocketing beyond the average collector's means, he is looking for a viable, valuable alternative. Doll artist dolls are made in small quantities for a very short period of time, are signed and dated and are by their nature, originals, never reproductions. Every desirable quality (except for age) that a collector could demand are intrinsic to an art doll. These have to be the collectors' items of the future.

In the last decade or so, doll artists have begun to band together in professional organizations which not only promote their work but act as guarantors of its quality and authenticity. Two such organizations are NIADA (National Institute of American Doll Artists), the premier organization of its kind, and ODACA (the Original Doll Artist Council of America), younger and larger. Both organizations boast of the high caliber of the work and ethical dealings of their members. There are also excellent artists who do not belong to any organization. They are more difficult to track down.

Recently there has been an explosion of interest in the miniatures field. Doll houses, tiny furniture and all aspects of the lilliputian

world have invaded the national consciousness. Grown-ups more than children appear affected by this mania, to the point of delightful obsession. These miniaturists embrace an exacting scale for their fancies. In that scale 1" = 1' (2.5cm = 30.5cm). For some reason, though, many miniaturists refuse to populate their fantasy worlds, preferring, perhaps, to imagine themselves therein. They give the excuse that any dolls available are just too clumsy, too unreal to fit their visions. I hope this book will change their minds.

Despite the recent growth in the field, there are relatively few doll artists who work in miniature. This is because of the above mentioned problems inherent in the production of miniatures. Fortunately, some doll artists do delight in the challenges of small scale work.

Not all dolls described herein are 1" = 1' (2.5cm = 30.5cm) scale. Some are smaller. Some are larger, but none is over 9in (22.9cm) in height. Some are "play" dolls, and some are

**Illustration I-5. CAROL NORDELL:** *Firebird.* Side view of Illustration I-4.

8

**Illustration I-6.** CAROL NORDELL: *Firebird.* Head-on view of Illustration I-4. Note how well balanced the sculpture's composition is from this viewpoint.

**Illustration I-7.** CAROL NORDELL: *Firebird.* Close-up of face. Note the neck and shoulder bones as the dancer appears to spread her arms.

kinfolk to Degas' ballerina, permanently fixed in position. It is my hope that in the years ahead, they, like Degas' ballerina, will at last gain the public acceptance they deserve.

### PLEASE NOTE:

I have purposely omitted addresses of all artists in this book for two reasons. The first is privacy. The second is permanency - - addresses are subject to change.

Doll artists who are affiliated with any of the major artist organizations can be contacted through them. Affiliations, where pertinent, are noted at the end of each profile. Please enclose a self-addressed stamped envelope (SASE) for a reply when writing for information.

### NIADA
(National Institute of American Doll Artists)
c/o Helen Bullard
303 Riley Street
Falls Church, Virginia 22046

### ODACA
(Original Doll Artist Council of America)
c/o Virginia Little, President
RD 1 Box 207
Beech Creek, Pennsylvania 16822

### IDMA
(International Doll Makers' Association)
c/o Betty Omohundro
3364 Pine Creek Drive
San Jose, California 95132

### NAME
(National Association of Miniature Enthusiasts)
1309 West Valencia
Suite H
Fullerton, California 92633

The work of doll artists described in this book is copyrighted by each individual doll artist. It is protected by United States statutes and may not be duplicated.

Many dolls in this book have been photographed next to an American penny to give an idea of their size. For those not familiar with American currency, a tracing of the size of this coin is provided below.

U.S.A.
ONE
CENT

**Color Illustration 16.** 1″ = 1′ scale (2.5cm = 30.5cm) *Lady, Child* and *Baby* by Mary Hoot. Polyform.

**Color Illustration 17.** 6in (15.2cm) *Father Christmas* by Beverly Port. Porcelain head and hands; glazed eyes. Wire armature in body. © 1980.

**Color Illustration 18.** 8½in (21.6cm) *Carrie O.* by Patricia Ryan Brooks. Hand-carved basswood head, arms and legs. Wire armature body. Human hair wig. ©1981.

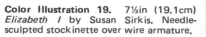

**Color Illustration 19.** 7½in (19.1cm) *Elizabeth I* by Susan Sirkis. Needle-sculpted stockinette over wire armature.

**Color Illustration 20.** 1″ = 1′ scale (2.5cm = 30.5cm) *Mlle Jou Jou de la Chambre* by Sheila Kwartler. Porcelain bisque shoulder plate with swivel head, lower limbs. Wire armatured cloth body. ©1981.

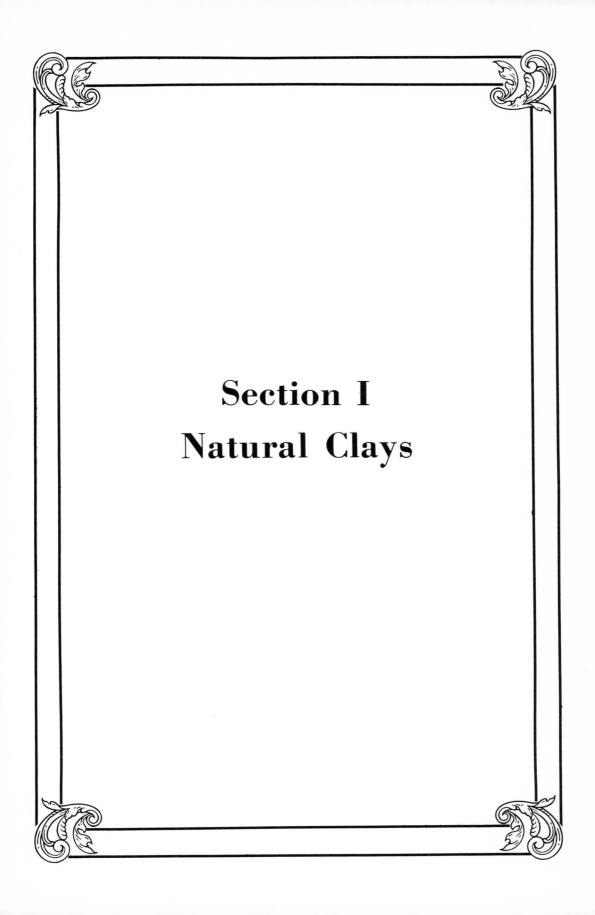

# Section I
# Natural Clays

Natural (water-based) clay was one of the earliest doll making materials. There are ancient Greek jointed dolls of fired clay which have survived the centuries. Clay is at once the easiest and the most difficult medium for the doll artist. Its malleability, its plasticity and its relative unpredictability provide the boundless pleasures and challenges which have made it the favorite medium of the American doll artist.

Clay is a relatively easy medium for sculpture. It is inexpensive and, if unfired, reusable. Even if it dries out, it can be reconstituted by the addition of water. It can be built up, added to, scraped away and thrown into a bucket for another day's work. When the sculpture is done, though, the clay cannot be left as it is, for it is too delicate: the sculpture is too easily lost. It must be fired or cast into another material.

Doll artists usually sculpt one of two types of clay. The first is natural, water-based clay. It may be a type of stoneware or terra-cotta or even porcelain. This clay can be left as it is, to gradually dry under close supervision, then polished up and fired in a kiln. It produces a one-of-a-kind doll, if a mold is not later on made of the piece.

The second type of clay is made using a natural clay as a base, but petroleum and some other elements are added which prevent the clay from drying out. This type of clay is a favorite of professional sculptors and is called, variously, plasticene or plastilina. It is usually grey or greenish-grey in color. Because of its oil content, it tends to be greasy. It comes in different hardnesses. Medium seems the best for making dolls. This clay seldom dries out. It cannot be fired. So molds must be made of sculptures made from this material. The sculptures must then be cast in another material.

Usually molds are made of plaster. Dental plaster or casting plaster are best. These molds must be used if clay or composition are used for casting the sculptures. If wax is used for the final product, a mold may be made of latex, also, with (usually) a plaster casing to hold it in place. Mold making is an art in itself. Most doll artists learn to make their own molds.

Different types of clay and different procedures can be used to reproduce a doll sculpture once a mold is made. First, one can press a clay, such as stoneware or porcelain, into a two-piece mold, let it set up, remove it and then seal the two sides together with more clay before the casting hardens. This is not always satisfactory.

Most doll makers use clay which has been liquified by the addition of water and (perhaps) some chemicals. This is called SLIP. Slip can be made of just about any natural clay. The most common ones for doll making are usually bought at ceramic supply houses.

There is a low-fire "ceramic" slip available which, in liquid form, is greyish. It fires to a chalky, porous white and is rather fragile. It must be "stained," or painted with china paints or glazed with ceramic glazes. Many people begin with this clay. Most graduate from it as it is limited in its uses. Its most practical use, many feel, is in making a "master sculpture" from a mold. An artist can pour his work in ceramic slip and fire it and then have a permanent master, in almost the same size as the original, from which he can make numerous successive molds.

Most doll artists work in porcelain, easily one of the most frustrating and fulfilling media available. Porcelain is the "Cadillac" of clays. It is extremely fine-grained. It can be used in several states of plasticity. In a liquid state, it is called slip and can be poured into molds and then decanted (turned upside down so that the liquid pours out again). This leaves a narrow scum on the inside of the mold which faithfully reproduces its details.

When the mold has set up for a while, it can then be opened carefully and the clay trimmed (fettled) and improved upon. When a casting is in this very soft state it can easily collapse or become warped, so great care must be used in its handling. This is the only time, however, when the clay can be safely perforated. So ears must be pierced and sew-holes and stringing-holes must be made at this stage. When it becomes harder, the clay will not permit this to be done.

**Illustration I-A.** Plastilina sculpture for head of *Amy Carter* doll, ©1977 by Carol-Lynn Waugh, in front of two-piece plaster mold made from that sculpture. Shown next to it is 1'' = 1' (2.5cm = 30.5cm) scale *Amy* reduction head, the result of successive reduction molds made from castings of the original sculpture.

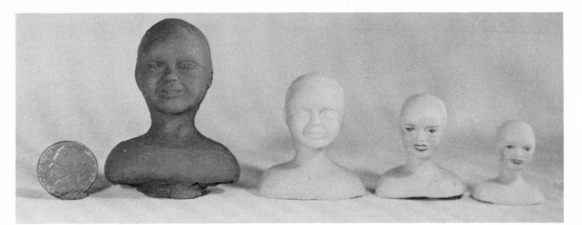

After it has been setting up for a while and it is neither wet nor dry, the clay is called "leather hard." At this point, curls and hairdos of porcelain may be added to the head, re-sculpting and polishing can be done, and the pieces can be fitted together tentatively on an all-bisque doll to see if they work.

When the clay is bone dry, it has to be one of the most delicate substances in the world. But it is at this state when it must be most handled. It has to be polished and repolished until it is free of any imperfections. Since the porcelain is far more delicate than egg shells at this state, it is often put into a kiln for a low (cone 019) firing before polishing.

This toughens it up and yet the clay can still be polished.

Porcelain is then fired to cone 6 (1859°F), which takes anywhere from two to fourteen hours, depending upon the kiln that is used. During firing the clay completely changes its qualities. It becomes hard and strong. In fact, to destroy their "seconds," some doll makers have been known to whack at them repeatedly with hammers.

Porcelain clay shrinks approximately 20 percent in the firing process. This results in an intensification of details that is very noticeable in dolls of a small scale. The fact that porcelain shrinks so much can be taken advantage of by the doll maker. He can make a sculpture in a scale much larger than the final product he wants, if he finds sculpting on a small model difficult. Then he can make a series of reduction molds from his sculpture to obtain the size doll desired.

A reduction mold is made in the following way. A head is sculpted in clay and a mold is made of it in plaster. This is poured in porcelain, decanted, polished, fired, and so forth. The head, after firing, is 20 percent (approximately, depending on the porcelain used) smaller than the original. Then, from *this* head a second mold, a reduction mold, is made. The head from this mold, after firing, will again be 20 percent smaller. This procedure can be continued ad nauseum. And this is the way the old manufacturers of bisque-headed dolls obtained dolls in so many sizes, all with the same heads.

The heads, after firing, are no longer porous and can hold water without glazing, unlike some other clays. At this stage, the heads are called BISQUE - - unglazed, but fired, clay. Any fired clay that is not glazed is called bisque, not just porcelain.

Illustration I-D. *Sarah/Andrew* by Helen McCook. Steps in reduction in size of porcelain heads. The unpainted porcelain bisque head at the left makes up into a 15in (38.1cm) doll. Doll at far right needs one more reduction to be doll house scale. The *Sarah* dolls have loops in their hair for insertion of a ribbon. ©

Most porcelain dolls nowadays are china painted. They used to be glazed all over, especially in the 19th century. This gave them a glassy appearance that looks like china dishes. Before china painting, they are polished to a uniform smoothness so that the china paint will not get caught in a rough, pitted surface. Sometimes it is refired to obtain a finer appearance.

China painting is an art in itself. In fact, the United States government has officially declared china painting to be a fine art, so it logically follows that anything using this technique might well also fall under this heading. So, perhaps, china painted porcelain dolls have achieved official government sanction as a fine art.

China painting is a difficult process, utilizing ground pigments that have a glass basis and oil vehicles for their mixing. Each color must be applied and fired separately in a kiln. Sometimes colors have to be reapplied and refired. Practice and experimentation are vital for this art. Colors can run or not fire properly, ruining the work. Most colors, especially the dark paints, are not removable after firing. Days and weeks of work can be spoiled by inaccurate china painting.

Working with porcelain may be hazardous to the health. The porcelain slip contains substances to which some people are allergic. It should be handled with waterproof gloves (surgical gloves are ideal), if for no other reason than its drying effect on some people's skin. During the polishing process, not only gloves, but a long-sleeved shirt, slacks, an apron and an industrial-strength breathing mask should be worn to limit skin and lung contact with the fine omnipresent powder of the clay dust. Prolonged breathing of the dust may be instrumental in causing silicosis in some individuals. Whatever contact one has with the substances in the dust seems to be cumulative. For this reason, porcelain should NEVER be put into the mouth in the unfired state, nor should china paints, some of which are lead-based. Lead is poisonous.

If a porcelain figure or doll or whatever survives all the steps involved in its creation and works the way it was intended to function, it is a source of immense pleasure and relief to its creator. The challenges involved in its production are both its lure and its bane for doll artists. And this is why porcelain dolls cost so much.

Illustration I-E. Unpainted porcelain bisque doll parts made by Helen McCook. This illustration gives a good idea of the way various doll parts are constructed. Note the sewing holes on the shoulder plates and the stringing holes on some of the arms, legs and bodies. At lower right are doll arms which have been reduced from the same original sculpture by use of reduction molds. These arms will be attached to fabric upper arms.

# 1. Carol Boyd Porcelain

Carol Boyd makes one-of-a-kind, individually modeled porcelain doll house dolls in the 1'' - 1' (2.5cm = 30.5cm) scale.

Her career as an original doll maker began around 1974, but her training in sculpture dates from the mid 1960s when she studied with a modern artist in Holland.

In the early 1970s, she began making large dolls from commercial molds. After refining her techniques, she started to make original dolls. Drawing on her background in arts, crafts, painting and sculpture, aided by her interest and skills in costuming derived from a theatre arts major, Carol is largely self-taught as a doll maker.

Her children and babies are usually all porcelain and jointed. The larger doll house dolls (older children and adults) have wired muslin bodies which are stuffed with polyester.

The lovely, realistic expressions and intricate costuming which falls naturally on their bodies are hallmarks of Boyd dolls. Most dolls wear Victorian clothing, as this is popular among doll house aficionadoes.

Whole families of mother, father, children, grandparents, maids, butlers, chauffeurs, gardeners and handymen are available. Some of Mrs. Boyd's most popular dolls are her all-porcelain babies, especially "screaming"

**Illustration 1-1.** 6in (12.7cm) *Veteran's Day.* Porcelain bisque head and lower limbs. Cloth body. 1980.

ones. She has made several sets of quintuplets, each with a different expression (sleeping, crying, laughing, and so forth).

Specialty dolls, such as portraits of people, a cellist to "play" a rare miniature cello, a well-dressed family of Victorian cats, a Eurasian beauty and tiny dolls to be held by doll house children all form part of the repertoire of this Virginia artist. Much of the fun in doll design, she states, comes from the research involved in producing a superior product. She is constantly reading, experimenting, searching for better techniques, unusual products and better ways of doing traditional tasks.

**Illustration 1-2.** 1'' = 1' (2.5cm = 30.5cm) scale *Family Portrait.* Porcelain bisque heads and lower limbs. Cloth bodies.

Illustration 1-4. 1" = 1' (2.5cm = 30.5cm) scale
*Screaming Baby.* All porcelain with movable limbs.

Illustration 1-3. 1" = 1' (2.5cm = 30.5cm) scale
*Victorian Lady.* Porcelain bisque head and lower
limbs. Cloth body.

The national awards she has won for her
work seem to indicate that this care in creation
is well worthwhile.

Carol Boyd dolls are signed and dated.

Carol Boyd is a member of the United
Federation of Doll Clubs (UFDC).

Illustration 1-5. 1" = 1' (2.5cm = 30.5cm) scale
*Victorian Girl.* Porcelain bisque head and lower limbs.
Cloth body.

**Illustration 1-6.** 1in (2.5cm) tall *Doll's Doll.* All porcelain bisque.

**Illustration 1-7.** 1" = 1' (2.5cm = 30.5cm) scale *Victorian Bride.* Porcelain bisque head and lower limbs. Cloth body.

# 2. Charlotte Byrd Porcelain

**Illustration 2-1.** Charlotte Byrd with early work. First row, left to right: *Little Squirt, Sidewalks of New York.* Second row: *Einstein, Christopher, Christina, Twickenham Belle.* ©

Charlotte Byrd of Huntsville, Alabama, began making dolls because of her genealogical research. When she would come to a dead end in tracing her ancestors' records at the local library, she would research antique porcelain dolls in her mother's growing collection. The siren call of the dolls was irresistible, but, as she had limited resources and an indomitable spirit, she decided to make her own dolls of porcelain rather than collect old ones.

Although she had a degree in illustration and had worked with Boeing as a technical illustrator and free lanced as a portrait artist for several years, she had had only one elemental course in sculpting, and this had been years before in college. Being of the belief that one can do anything he sets his mind to if he wants it badly enough, she taught herself to make dolls. Her method was familiar to most doll artists, trial and error.

Gradually she learned the tricks of the craft, that clay models must be hollowed out before firing or they explode, for instance.

She taught herself mold making and porcelain pouring and firing. She says, "I developed a healthy respect for all original doll artists and the tremendous amounts of time and care they go through to produce one doll."

By 1981, Mrs. Byrd had produced 14 original dolls. Six of them are under 9in (22.9cm) in size, and they show how well her many efforts have paid off.

She strives for happy, smiling, "glowing" faces that show the inner character of her dolls rather than their outward beauty. They represent children of times gone by: 1905 in *The Sidewalks of New York,* the 1920s in *Scooter,* the 1890s in *The Bubble Blower* and the 1960s in the baby from *Special Moments,* a scene which depicts a father holding a baby in a hammock. The larger dolls are also nostalgic: *Twickenham Belle,* a 17-year-old Southern Belle wears an 1850s ballgown.

**Illustration 2-2.** 6½in (16.5cm) *Bubble Blower.* All-bisque swivel-neck 1890s girl. © July 1980.

**Illustration 2-3.** 6½in (16.5cm) - - each doll. *Sidewalks of New York.* Mechanical group of 1905-era children jumping rope. *Nathan* (dressed in sailor suit) and *Alicia* (holding other end of rope) have porcelain swivel head shoulder plates and limbs, cloth bodies which hold jump rope mechanism. *Mary Beth* is all bisque with swivel head. Created in 1979 for UFDC convention held in New York City. ©

*Christopher* and *Christina* are 13in (33.0cm) toddlers of the 1940s. *Einstein in Later Years* is Mrs. Byrd's first portrait work and shows the scientist in the 1950s.

Byrd dolls have a sense of arrested motion, of activity in progress that reminds one of 19th century genre paintings. Indeed, some of the dolls are geared for motion. *The Sidewalks of New York* scene is a mechanical group featuring three 6½in (16.5cm) rope-jumping children: *Nathan, Marybeth* and *Alicia. Marybeth* jumps when a handle is turned. The rigging of this setup took 300 hours. *Special Moments* makes use of a movable green hammock for its impact.

Mrs. Byrd's dolls are sculpted in plasticene clay, polyform clay or ceramic clay. Editions are poured of porcelain. Her small dolls are all porcelain, with the exception of the two dolls holding the jump rope in *Sidewalks of New York* who have cloth bodies.

**Illustration 2-4.** 5½in (14.0cm) *Baby* from *Special Moments* group. All-bisque 7-month-old baby with swivel neck. Fully jointed. Wears pastel play suit. Created June, 1980. © *Photograph by Buel Case Studios.*

**Illustration 2-5.** 5½in (14.0cm) *Baby* from *Special Moments* group. All-bisque 7-month-old baby with swivel neck. Fully jointed. Wearing christening gown. Lies on matching pillow. ©

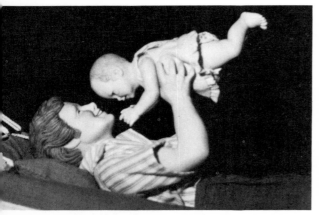

**Illustration 2-6.** 5½in (14.0cm) *Baby* from *Special Moments* group held by father (close-up of group showing "communication" between father and child). Created for Father's Day, June, 1980. ©

The small dolls have all-bisque construction with swivel necks and movable arms and legs which are jointed at shoulder and hips, respectively. They are held together with elastic cord. Some have sculpted hair. This is done when the hairstyle desired is too short for Mrs. Byrd to easily make a wig. An example of this is *Scooter* with his short windswept

**Illustration 2-7.** 6½in (16.5cm) *Scooter.* All-bisque swivel-neck 7-year-old boy from 1920s era riding his red scotter. Created July, 1980.©

barber cut and the smiling 5½in (14.0cm) baby. Others have small mohair wigs on tiny base caps of tightly woven nylon. The hair is hand-stitched in rows and styled, then applied to the doll's bald pate head.

In costuming the dolls, Mrs. Byrd uses the finest available materials: silks, old laces, Swiss batiste, linens and Pendleton wools. To keep quality up, dolls are only available dressed. Natural fibers are used, as they are much easier to sew when making rolled hems, French seams, darts and tucks in tiny dresses. Most of the costumes are hand-stitched. The artist feels the costume is an important part of creating the total feeling in the doll. She tries to make it as authentic as she can.

Mrs. Byrd's dolls are sold in limited editions. An edition of an individual doll is 12. She never makes more than 15 dolls from any of her group settings (she sells these dolls individually, as well as in the group), then closes out the edition so she can go on to new things.

Charlotte Byrd's dolls are marked in the following ways:
1.  Shoulder plate dolls:
    between holes on the front - -
    © Original Charlotte Byrd
    at lower edge of back - -
    edition number or doll, Charlotte Byrd, date, sometimes doll name
2.  Swivel neck dolls:
    signed under base of skull rear - -
    Original (edition number), Charlotte Byrd, date

Charlotte Byrd is a member of the United Federation of Doll Clubs (UFDC) and the Original Doll Artist Council of America (ODACA).

# 3. Susan Fosnot Clay

Susan Fosnot's jointed miniature dolls and bears are creatures of the imagination. They are individually sculpted of various tinted ceramic clays, fired and painted. Each one embodies a small message from its creator.

Through her miniature creatures, the Wisconsin artist tries to express something about living, about what it is to be very small: a small doll, a small child, a small being in a very large world.

Susan Fosnot was born in Madison, Wisconsin, in 1953. As a child she loved making things, especially tiny things. She crafted her first dolls before kindergarten. In art school (University of Wisconsin), she made masks and drawings. By a quirk of fate she attended a doll show and realized the myriad of possibilities involved in the doll as an art form. The combination of many media with the fascination of the idea behind the doll itself - - as a magic and fantasy object - - had great appeal to her.

From the start Susan wanted to make her dolls different from those of others. So she set off on a series of experiments, many of them

**Illustration 3-2.** 3½in (8.9cm) *Babies*. Bisque. Jointed at arms and legs with wire. Note jointing on *Bald Baby*, upper left. *Black Baby* shows variety of skin tone. It is one of very few dressed miniatures. He has glass eyes and a soft body. Japanese girl has Japanese-style sandals. Signed: FOSNOT.

tragic, until she found materials which would work together. She has made dolls succsssfully from many media, ranging from a series of 30in (76.2cm) painted fabric dolls to ceramic babies less than 2in (5.1cm) tall.

Her miniature dolls are of hand-formed ceramic. Each one is a one-of-a-kind made without molds. This allows for very fine detail and a freshness of expression that Ms. Fosnot finds lacking in mold-produced dolls. She has developed a means to color the clay bodies she uses to obtain a variety of complexion hues which are integral to the clay.

The dolls are generally made with head and body in one piece and the arms and legs separate. She has a method of jointing the legs which makes them flexible and allows the dolls to have shapely behinds. Her dolls have what a friend of hers terms "working bodies."

**Illustration 3-1.** 3½in (8.9cm) *Fat Boy* and *Bald Baby*. Bisque. Jointed at arms and legs with wire. *Fat Boy* wears glasses of wire. Signed: FOSNOT.

**Illustration 3-3.** 1" = 1' (2.5cm = 30.5cm) scale *Dollhouse Children.* The infant is less than 2in (5.1cm) long. All bisque. Jointed with wires. Girl has lamb skin wig. Signed: FOSNOT.

**Illustration 3-4.** 3½in (8.9cm) *Babies.* Bisque. Jointed with wire. Babies on left and right have alpaca hair. Signed: FOSNOT.

Dolls are fired in her tiny kiln (the interior dimension is one cubic foot). Then they are china painted or cold painted and jointed with wire. Some of them have hair of natural fiber such as lamb's wool or alpaca.

"For me," she says, "the dolls are complete at this point - - only rarely do I dress them. They are intended to be naked like the 'Venus de Milo' or the cherubs in Baroque art."

Her dolls vary in concept from the realistic to the fantastic. At one end of the spectrum are portrait dolls, at the other, blue cherubs. The portraits are of children and adults: friends, acquaintances and patrons. She also makes

miniature children that are not portraits. Each possesses a personality all its own. Often they are children of ethnic minorities: a bald and surly Chinese baby, a chubby Japanese girl, a wide-eyed black girl with pigtails and bows, a white boy with freshly combed hair who is not too happy about it.

And then there are her teddies. In each she tries to discover a little different teddy bear personality: sad, confused, stupid, sleepy.

**Illustration 3-5.** 6in (15.2cm) *College Professor.* Ceramic bisque. Five-piece jointed body. Anatomically correct. Sculpted beard and hair.

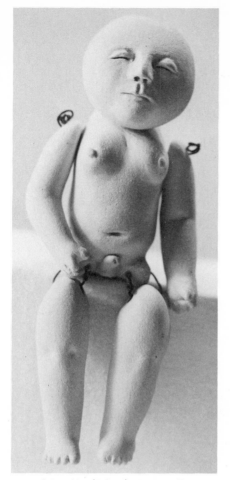

From the teddies it is not such a great leap to her less realistic dolls. They are beings from a fantasy world. Susan strives to give them more presence as independent objects by making them less of a representation of something other than what they are. Each one represents only itself and is, therefore, more complete and does not try to be a real person. She calls them cherubs and angels. They are a lovely pale blue, about 3in (7.6cm) tall, of babyish proportions and forms. They have mask-like moon faces and are hermaphroditic. "They are lovely but they are also repellant," the artist describes them.

Susan Fosnot is active in the Wisconsin art world. She participates in fine arts shows and says, "Doll making IS joining the ranks of painting and sculpture."

Susan Fosnot dolls are signed FOSNOT, usually on the side.

**Illustration 3-6.** 3in (7.6cm) *Cherub.* Blue bisque. Jointed with wire.

**Illustration 3-7.** 2in (5.1cm) *Grumpy Bear.* Terracotta bisque. Jointed with wire. Felt vest attached to body when arm wires inserted. *Carol-Lynn Rössel Waugh Collection.*

**Illustration 3-8.** Various Sizes: *Bears.* (Compare with size of coin.) Bisque. Jointed with wires. Signed: FOSNOT.

# 4. Herta Foster Porcelain

**Illustration 4-1.** 1" = 1' (2.5cm = 30.5cm) scale *Susanna*. Porcelain head and hands. Padded fabric body over copper wire frame. Mohair hair.

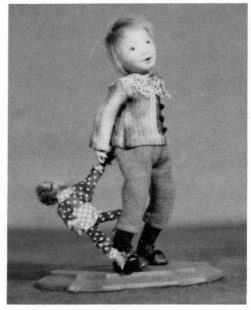

**Illustration 4-2.** 1" = 1' (2.5cm = 30.5cm) scale *Leonard with Punch*. Porcelain head and hands. Padded fabric body over copper wire frame. Mohair hair.

Herta Foster's father and grandfather were artists, sculptors, painters, restorers and art collectors. It was a foregone conclusion that she should try some sort of art, but World War II intervened.

In 1944, when she was a teenager in Germany, her family lost its house, studios, collections and all. While displaced, young Herta made use of her fine arts training. She designed and made stuffed animals of velvet drapes donated by friends to sell or trade for food. Thus began her career as a doll designer.

After marriage and after the war she moved to California. She has made dolls, puppets, miniatures and marionettes, the latter for professional puppeteers, for many years. Using her own characters and animals, she illustrated a children's book, *Gregg Finds an Egg,* by Sarah Keyser, in 1972, by means of color photographs.

In 1960, she started making 14in (35.6cm) tall satirical figures, porcelain children and

**Illustration 4-3.** 1" = 1' (2.5cm = 30.5cm) scale *Lucille* (left) and *Priscilla* (on chair). Porcelain heads and hands. Padded fabric bodies over copper wire frames. Mohair hair.

fully-jointed felt children. The latter were about 12in (30.5cm) tall, standing. In 1975 she started making her "miniettes," as she calls the tiniest of her dolls. They are approximately 1" = 1' (2.5cm = 30.5cm) scale. Sometimes they turn out a bit larger, but not visually so.

These little children have heads and arms of porcelain. The rest of the body is made up over a copper wire frame. The body is shaped with cotton padding and wrapped with tiny strips of thin white cotton material. The legs are made right over the wire with stockings and shoes put onto the finished, shaped leg. The upper arms are also wire with the porcelain lower arms attached to them.

Hair on Foster dolls is mohair or human hair.

Clothing is sewn directly on top of the doll's body. The costumes depend on the artist's fancy. She does not specialize in any one era. Some are period costumes, some modern and some just "old fashioned."

To date (1981), she has designed 16 different "miniettes," with limited editions of ten each. But she has never made that many of any of them because she tires of making any doll too often. She has discontinued several after two or three. None look the same, though, even in multiples.

They are usually made only fully dressed with accessories (which the artist almost always makes herself).

Eventually, as time permits, Mrs. Foster wants to create some small adult period figures close to or slightly larger than the "one inch" scale.

Herta Foster is a member of the United Federation of Doll Clubs (UFDC) and the National Institute of American Doll Artists (NIADA).

**Illustration 4-5.** 1" = 1' (2.5cm = 30.5cm) scale *Christopher.* Porcelain head and hands. Padded fabric body over copper wire frame. Mohair hair.

**Illustration 4-6.** 1" = 1' (2.5cm = 30.5cm) scale *Jessica.* Porcelain head and hands. Padded fabric body over copper wire frame. Mohair hair.

**Illustration 4-4.** 1" = 1' (2.5cm = 30.5cm) scale *Heidi.* Porcelain head and hands. Padded fabric body over copper wire frame. Mohair hair.

# 5. Jan and Lyn Gabrielson Porcelain

**Illustration 5-1.** 7½in (19.1cm) *Miss Muffett.* All porcelain. Jointed at head, shoulders and legs. Openings for head and limbs lined with kid leather. Mohair wig. Close-up detail of porcelain teardrop. ©1980.

Jan and Lyn Gabrielson are a mother and daughter team who combine their skills to produce delightful nursery rhyme characters of high-fire porcelain bisque.

Although each is capable of doing a complete doll, they enjoy the working combination that they have established. And they work at it 12 to 18 hours a day, six days a week. They share the tasks of construction. Jan, Lyn's mother, sculpts the dolls. Lyn makes the molds, pours, cleans, fires and paints the dolls. They both line the doll joints and string the dolls. Jan designs and makes the costumes as well as the wigs to complete them.

This partnership started by accident when in May, 1979, Lyn accompanied a friend to a doll show and fell in love with the original dolls there. Since both women were already artists working with oil painting, china painting, charcoals and pastels, they decided to give dolls a try even though Jan, the present sculptor of the team, had at that point never picked up a piece of clay.

The dolls range from 1in (2.5cm) to 15in (38.1cm) tall and are almost exclusively porcelain. Some of the tiniest ones are made of Sculpey (polyform). The porcelain dolls are all bisque, jointed at the head, shoulders and legs. The openings for the head and limbs are lined with kid leather. Their wigs are mainly mohair.

These children are as realistic as possible, but Jan still wants them to look like dolls,

not statues. She strives for perfection when sculpting. Each piece must be accurate and anatomically correct. Everything is measured and remeasured to certify this.

The team has made about 25 different miniature dolls. Their 4¼in (10.9cm) dolls are basically one-of-a-kind. They try to do individual dolls for people. If a customer wants a specific time period, expression, hair color or stance, they try to be accommodating. Their nursery rhyme characters are limited editions of 50 each.

The Gabrielsons' nursery rhyme characters have distinctive personalities. *Bo Peep* is very sad and dressed as a lowly country shepherdess. *Jack Horner* is a happy little rich boy dressed in silk and satin. *Miss Muffett* is an elegant little rich girl frightened by a spider and *Wee Willie Winkie* is a small town crier dressed in a night shirt ready for "running through the town."

The dolls are costumed in styles from several eras. Both *Jack Horner* and *Wee Willie Winkie* wear 1780s styles. *Bo Peep* and *Miss Muffett* have Victorian and Edwardian fashions. Other dolls wear contemporary clothes, "old fashioned" clothes and ones from the 1950s.

Nursery rhyme characters are only available fully dressed. Other dolls not in limited editions are available fully dressed or undressed.

Gabrielson dolls are marked on the back of the head:

> J & L Gabrielson
> ©year copyrighted.

Jan and Lyn Gabrielson are members of the United Federation of Doll Clubs (UFDC), the Original Doll Artist Council of America (ODACA) and the International Doll Makers Association (IDMA).

**Illustration 5-2.** Left to Right: 7½in (19.1cm) tall *Jack Horner,* © 1979; *Wee Willie Winkie,* © 1980; *Bo Peep,* © 1979; *Miss Muffett,* ©1979. Center doll: 4in (10.2cm) one-of-a-kind doll. All porcelain. Jointed at head, shoulders and legs. Openings for head and limbs lined with kid leather. Mohair wigs.

# 6. Donna Guinn Porcelain

**Illustration 6-1.** Donna Guinn with some of her original dolls.

Donna Guinn's interest in dolls and in art dates from her childhood. In 1976, these two interests collaborated for the creation of her first two original dolls, the 11in (27.9cm) tall *Country Craig* and *Country Kate.*

She had been making dolls from a variety of materials since she was young. Cloth, wood, modeling and "kitchen clays," pipe cleaners, papier-mâché; all these were tried until the upstate New Yorker became involved with various ceramic derivatives and found that this was the medium in which she could best express herself.

Her doll business evolved as a result of numerous ceramic classes and seminars followed by research in the art of mold making. She started at the Norwich, New York, library, persued articles in doll publications and closely examined professional molds.

She has been making miniature dolls (8in [20.3cm] or less) commercially since 1978 when she created her first children, *Kim* and *Eric,* who are named after Mrs. Guinn's grandchildren. They are 5½in (14.0cm) tall and have their own Small World of Play Cottage and furniture which the artist also designed for them.

**Illustration 6-2.** 6in (15.2cm) *Eric* and *Kim.* Porcelain shoulder plates and lower limbs. Cloth bodies. Mohair wigs.

**Illustration 6-3.** 6in (15.2cm) *Kim.* Close-up of Illustration 2.

These dolls were designed to be children of the 1920s. Her first originals represent teenagers during the Lincoln era. *Suk,* a Korean miss, is 16in (40.6cm) tall, and an annual series of Christmas ornament dolls is 3½in (8.9cm) tall.

*Kim* and *Eric* are cast of porcelain bisque slip. They have soft bodies made of a sturdy flesh-colored fabric stuffed with sawdust. Their limbs are porcelain and movable, and they bend at the knees. This combination was used so they would be easily maneuverable in the Play Cottage and capable of sitting in the furniture which is built of sturdy wood and scaled 1" = 1' (2.5cm = 30.5cm). The dolls and their Small World were designed to encourage creative play in which children can easily imagine themselves as *Kim* and *Eric* in the little cottage.

Each doll wears a mohair wig and is available in a kit or finished, in caucasian or black.

**Illustration 6-5.** *Kim and Eric's Playhouse* by Donna Guinn. 6in (15.2cm) *Kim* doll inside.

**Illustration 6-4.** 6in (15.2cm) *Eric.* Close-up of Illustration 2.

The Santa's helpers Christmas ornament dolls range from 3½in to 3¾in (8.9cm to 9.6cm) in height and are made entirely of Dresden transluscent porcelain, even the hair. They have movable arms and stand by themselves on sturdy child-like legs. They are dressed in wintery velvets, "furs" and plaids and have special little matching velvet loops fastened at the back for insertion of an ornament hanger so they can be palced onto a Christmas tree.

Donna Guinn's dolls are not strictly realistic, abstract characterizations or historical in nature but a kind of combination of all of these descriptions.

A great deal of research goes into the costuming of Guinn dolls. Then Mrs. Guinn does her own designing, pattern making, selection of fabric and sewing.

Each of Donna Guinn's dolls' heads carries her logo, initials and date on the back of the chest plate, along with copyright notice. When a customer orders an assembled doll rather than a kit, it is signed and dated along the back on the body. If the customer orders a finished doll (assembled and dressed), it is signed and dated along the back of the body, and Mrs. Guinn's personal label is sewn into the garment.

Donna Guinn is a member of the United Federation of Doll Clubs (UFDC), the Original Doll Artist Council of America (ODACA), the International Doll Makers Association (IDMA) and the Doll Artisan Guild (DAG).

**Illustration 6-8.** 3½in (8.9cm) *Charlotte.* Close-up of Illustration 6-7 doll. ©1980.

**Illustration 6-6.** Donna Guinn sculpting plastilina head of her doll, *Suk.*

**Illustration 6-9.** 3½in (8.9cm) *June.* Close-up of Illustration 6-7 doll. ©1981.

**Illustration 6-7.** 3½in (8.9cm) *Charlotte* and *June.* All-porcelain Christmas ornament dolls for 1980 and 1981, respectively. One-piece head-torso-legs. Movable arms. Dressed in velvet ribbons and imitation fur trims. Sculpted, china painted hair. Hanger loop at back of neck on each doll.

# 7. Jean Heighton
## Porcelain and Ceramic Clay

**Illustration 7-1.** 6in (15.2cm) *Porcina Rosebud.* All porcelain. Jointed at head, arms and legs. Set-in eyes.

Jean Heighton has one of the best senses of humor in the American doll world. One look at her output will convince the viewer.

Her *Fantasy Folk* are incongruent juxtapositions of animals and fairy tales. These creatures take on human characteristics and dignity in a most plausible way under implausible circumstances. Their imaginative costuming sets off their personas with a flair.

Their names are a roll call of wonder: *Red Riding Rat, Porcina Rosebud, Bye Baby Bunting* (a small pigbaby in blanket and lace covered basket), *Ballerina Frog, Ballerina Pachyderma, Porcina Pokebonnet* (a mother pig with babe-in-arms) and *Froggy-went-a-Courting.* These and well-dressed rabbit and goat families form only a part of the menagerie; there are about 35 animals in all.

Among the human characters the California artist has designed are *Mother Goose, Sherlock Holmes, Abraham* and *Mary Todd Lincoln,* Indians of all tribes, *Santa, Mrs. Claus,*

*Father Christmas, Tevye* from "Fiddler on the Roof," *Eloise, Henry* and the fifteen-piece all bisque "naughty ladies."

All Heighton dolls are designed, dressed and entirely made by the artist. Some have soft (felt and wire armature) bodies; some are all bisque.

*Fantasy Folk* are done in either "ceramic" or high-fire porcelain slipcast bisque. At times, eyes, teeth and tongues are set in.

Their size ranges from the 3in (7.6cm) *Bye Baby Bunting* piglet to 9in (22.9cm) tall in porcelain bisque for the tall animal people.

There is a minor controversy in the doll world over whether animal dolls should be considered as true dolls since they are not really human. After viewing the work of Jean Heighton, it is nearly impossible to deny these critters their humanity.

Jean Heighton's dolls are signed in the following way:

"Jean Heighton" is signed if there is room, the symbol 𝓗 , if not. The symbol is used on heads. If the doll wears shoes, one may have a capital "J," the other an "H."

Jean Heighton is a member of the Continental Doll Artisans Guild of California and the Peninsula Doll Artists' Association of California.

**Illustration 7-2.** 6in (15.2cm) *Porcina Piglets.* All porcelain. Jointed at head, arms and legs. Set-in eyes. Dressed in eyelet baby dresses.

**Illustration 7-3.** 9in (22.9cm) *Mr. and Mrs. Rabbit* and 3in (7.6cm) *New Baby.* Porcelain heads, hands and feet. Wire and felt stuffed bodies. Set-in eyes.

**Illustration 7-5.** 9in (22.9cm) *Red Riding Rat.* Porcelain head and lower limbs. Wire and felt stuffed body. Set-in eyes.

**Illustration 7-4.** 9in (22.9cm) *Ballerina Pachyderma.* Ceramic head and lower limbs. Wire and felt stuffed body. Set-in eyes.

**Illustration 7-6.** 9in (22.9cm) *Ballerina Frog.* Green ceramic head and lower limbs. Wire and felt stuffed body.

**Illustration 7-9.** 3in (7.6cm) *Bye Baby Bunting.* All porcelain.

**Illustration 7-7.** 9in (22.9cm) *Froggie-went-a-Courting.* Green ceramic head and lower limbs. Wire and felt stuffed body.

**Illustration 7-10.** 5¾in (14.7cm) *Naughty Ladies.* Fifteen-piece all porcelain construction. Jointed at heads, shoulders, elbows, wrists, waist, hips, knees and feet. Set-in eyes. Mohair wigs. © 1981.

**Illustration 7-8.** 9in (22.9cm) *Porcien Pokebonnet* and 3in (7.6cm) *Bye Baby Bunting. Porcien Pokebonnet* has ceramic head and lower limbs, wire and felt stuffed body, set-in eyes. *Bye Baby Bunting* is all porcelain.

**Illustration 7-11.** 7¾in (19.8cm) *Eloise* and *Henry.* All porcelain dolls. Open mouths with set-in teeth and tongue. Set-in eyes. Human hair wigs. © 1981.

**Illustration 7-12.** 5¾in (14.7cm) *Naughty Ladies.* Fifteen-piece all-porcelain construction. Jointed at heads, shoulders, elbows, wrists, waist, hips, knees and feet. Set-in eyes. Mohair wigs. © 1981.

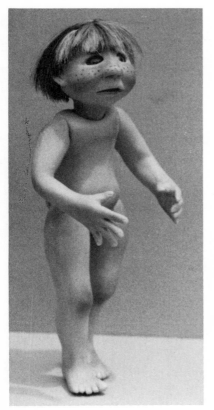

**Illustration 7-13.** 7¾in (19.8cm) *Henry.* All porcelain. Open mouth with set-in teeth and tongue. Set-in eyes. Human hair wig. © 1981.

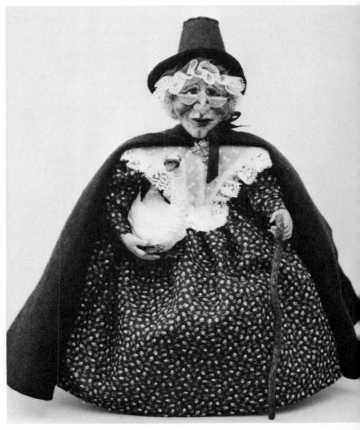

**Illustration 7-14.** 9in (22.9cm) *Mother Goose.* Ceramic bisque head and lower limbs. Felt and wire stuffed body. Holding ceramic goose.

# 8. Janna Joseph Porcelain

Janna Joseph recreates Hollywood in miniature. She specializes in portrait dolls made of slipcast porcelain bisque. The majority of her dolls are of 1'' = 1' (2.5cm = 30.5cm) scale or smaller.

She has been working in porcelain since 1978 and has created since that time an extensive cast of characters representing stars of the large and small screen. In Janna Joseph's world, *Arnold,* the little boy from television's "Different Strokes" program, can sit down and play with a six-year-old *Shirley Temple,* who has her own *Shirley Temple* dolls, although their counterparts in the real world are generation gaps apart.

Almost the whole cast of "Gone With the Wind" is here: *Rhett, Scarlett* (available in four different outfits), *Melanie, Ashley, Mammy* and *Bonnie Blue. Mae West, John Wayne, Marilyn Monroe* and *Dolly Parton* share the stage with *Nelson Eddy* and *Jeanette MacDonald* and *J. R. Ewing* as played by Larry Hagman on the television show, "Dallas." Famous fictional celebrities are *Sherlock Holmes, Dr. Watson, Snow White, Eloise* and *Dorothy* and *Toto* from "The Wizard of Oz."

The North Carolina artist also makes extensive doll house families, both white and black.

Her "dolly dolls" are 3in (7.6cm) and under in height. These are all porcelain, as opposed to the cloth-bodied construction of most of the larger dolls.

Bears are also important personages for Mrs. Joseph. Each has a distinct name and personality which has been set out for him to enact. For example: *Dr. Brownie Bear* and *Nurse Bonnie* are 2in (5.1cm) tall brown porcelain bears. *Dr. Brownie* has his little black bag, bow tie and stethoscope. *Nurse Bonnie* has her nurse's cap and white apron. She also has a crush on *Dr. Brownie.* Mrs. Joseph always sells them as a set because they cannot bear to be parted. *Bobby Bear* is a little boy bear with a molded-on sailor suit and a slightly wicked expression. Then there are, of course, *Teddy* and *Theodora,* *Scatlett O'Beara* and *Rhett Beartler* make up the Hollywood contingent.

These dolls have a freshness and liveliness that is charming. The portraits, especially, capture a small bit of the American dream.

**Illustration 8-1.** 2in (5.1cm) *Dr. Brownie* and *Nurse Bonnie.* All porcelain brown bears. Jointed with wire at arms and legs. *Dr. Brownie* has his little black bag, bow tie and stethoscope. *Nurse Bonnie* has her nurse's cap, white apron, and a crush on *Dr. Brownie.* They cannot bear to be separated.

**Illustration 8-2.** 6in (15.2cm) *Santa* and 4½in (11.5cm) *Shirley* with her 2in (5.1cm) *Shirley* doll. *Santa* and *Shirley* have porcelain shoulder plates and lower limbs, cloth bodies. *Shirley* doll is jointed, all porcelain. Mohair wigs.

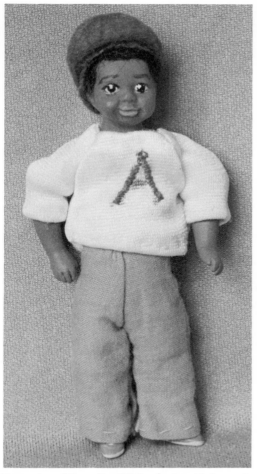

**Illustration 8-3.** 4in (10.2cm) *Arnold* from the television show, "Different Strokes." Porcelain bisque shoulder plate and lower limbs. Cloth body. Mohair wig.

**Illustration 8-4.** 6in (15.2cm) *Rhett Butler* and 5½in (14.0cm) *Scarlett O'Hara.* Porcelain shoulder plates and lower limbs. Fabric bodies. Mohair wigs.

Janna Joseph dolls are signed on the back of the shoulder plate or on the back of the head, for swivel-head dolls: JJ/date. If the doll is a limited edition, the number, for example 06/30, is also included.

Janna Joseph is a member of the United Federation of Doll Clubs (UFDC), the National Association of Miniature Enthusiasts (NAME) and the International Doll Makers Association (IDMA).

**Illustration 8-5.** 3in (7.6cm) and smaller: *Bears* and *Dolls.* All porcelain jointed toys. The *Gibson Girl* at middle of lower shelf is 3in (7.6cm) tall. The others range from 1½in (3.8cm) to 2½in (6.4cm) in height.

**Illustration 8-7.** 1½in (3.8cm) *Sailor Bears.* All porcelain five-piece construction. Jointed with nichrome wire. Molded-on sailor suits. China painted.

**Illustration 8-6.** 4½in (11.5cm) *Shirley Temple.* Porcelain shoulder plate and lower limbs. Cloth body. Mohair wig. Dressed in the pink organdy costume from the movie, "The Little Colonel."

**Illustration 8-8.** *Doll Hospital Room* display showing a variety of Janna Joseph's miniature dolls and animals.

**Illustration 8-9.** 4½in (11.5cm) *Peggy* and 1½in (3.8cm) *Doll House Doll's Doll. Peggy* has porcelain shoulder plate and lower limbs. Cloth body. Doll is all porcelain.

**Illustration 8-10.** 1¾in (4.5cm) *Tallulah* and *Tabitha* by Janna Joseph. All porcelain, china painted cat dolls. Molded-on shirts with painted bows and collars, molded bows in hair. Elastic strung. Pleated gingham skirts. ©1981.

Illustration 8-11. Approximately 2in (5.1cm) *Baby Ronnie* by Janna Joseph. All porcelain jointed body. China painted. Elastic strung. Crocheted pram suit, hat and blanket not by the artist.

Illustration 8-13. 5in (12.7cm) *Aunt Pitty Pat* by Janna Joseph. China painted porcelain shoulder plate, lower limbs. Wire armatured cloth body. Mohair wig.

Illustration 8-14. 5in (12.7cm) *Nēdra Volz as seen in her role of "Adelaide" on the television program "Different Strokes"* by Janna Joseph. China painted porcelain shoulder plate, lower limbs. Wire armatured cloth body. Mohair wig. Dressed in Oriental lounging pajamas. ©1981.

Illustration 8-12. 5in (12.7cm) *Prissy (Butterfly McQueen) from "Gone With the Wind"* by Janna Joseph. Medium brown china painted porcelain shoulder plate, lower limbs. Wire armatured cloth body. Mohair wig.

Illustration 8-15. 5in (12.7cm) *Nēdra Volz* by Janna Joseph. Close-up of Illustration 8-14.

39

Illustration 8-16. 5½in (14.0cm) *Jane Withers as an adult* and 4in (10.2cm) *Jane Withers as a child* by Janna Joseph. China painted porcelain bisque limbs and shoulder plates. Wire armatured cloth covered bodies. Mohair wigs. Dressed in blue jeans and gingham shirts. Young Jane Withers wears straw hat and carries brown fuzzy teddy bear. ©1981.

Illustration 8-18. 5-7/8in (14.9cm) *Ernestine, the Erte' Model* by Janna Joseph. China painted porcelain bisque shoulder plate, swivel head, arms and lower legs. Wire armatured cloth covered body. Mohair wig. ©1981.

Illustration 8-19. 5-7/8in (14.9cm) *Ernestine, the Erte' Model* by Janna Joseph. Detail of Illustration 8-18.

Illustration 8-17. 4in (10.2cm) *Jane Withers as a child* by Janna Joseph. Detail of Illustration 8-16.

Illustration 8-20. Janna Joseph. Photograph taken December 31, 1981.

# 9. Sheila Kwartler
# Porcelain, Polyform

Sheila Kwartler's miniature people are very real. One day she was in an antiques shop looking for minute period trims to embellish her tiny dolls' clothes. She introduced herself to the owner and explained what she was interested in. To give a general idea of the type of dolls she made, she showed the proprietor a photograph of her 1" = 1' (2.5cm = 30.5cm) scale *Dr. Watson* doll. The woman looked at the photograph, then at her, very confused. "I don't understand," she replied. "I make doll house dolls," the artist answered. "I still don't understand," the shopkeeper repeated. "He's only 5¾in (14.7cm) tall," the artist explained patiently. "You mean this is a doll?" exclaimed the antique dealer. She had thought the photograph was of a real person. Sheila's dolls are like that.

And they are very real to her. "I'm in trouble if I don't know what they're saying to each other, even before I make them," she once confided. But she does. And she puts her dolls into little animated vignettes so that the rest of the world can share their secrets, too.

**Illustration 9-2.** 5¾in (12.2cm) *Doctor Watson.* Polyform head and lower limbs. Padded wire armature body.

**Illustration 9-1.** 6in (15.2cm) *Sherlock Holmes.* Polyform head and lower limbs. Padded wire armature body.

**Illustration 9-3.** *Holmes* and *Watson.* Composite of Illustrations 9-1 and 9-2.

**Illustration 9-4.** 5½in (16.5cm) *Lilly*. Polyform head and lower limbs. Padded wire armature body. Mohair hair.

**Illustration 9-5.** 6in (15.2cm) *Dan*. Polyform head and lower limbs. Padded wire armature body.

The first dolls the New Yorker designed, in 1979, were for a gala ball staged in her doll house mansion's grand ballroom. Although she had had extensive art training, she had never sculpted or made a doll, except for childhood efforts. But her instincts and sense of proportion led her to make the right choices of media and technique. Her first dolls were a smashing success. So was the ball. Its guest list grew and grew. Since it was staged in the late 19th century, *Sherlock Holmes* and *Dr. Watson*

were invited to give the party an intellectual air.

These dolls soon made their way to the permanent collection of the Museum of the City of New York via exhibition in a museum show, "Toys for Adults." They had to be cloned to return to the ball.

The success of the detective duo led Mrs. Kwartler to the creation of more literary characters. One of the most popular of these is a sensuous, romanticized *Dracula* who hovers over his bride.

Although she began porcelain production in 1981, Sheila's early dolls were made of polyform. Her doll making techniques for the two types of dolls are very similar, although the later dolls go a step further. A mold is made from the original sculptures for making duplicates.

The earlier dolls' heads, breast plates, forearms, hands, calves and feet were individually sculpted of polyform into which wires were inserted to form the body armature. After baking, the sculpted parts were painted with acrylics, signed and dated and then covered with serveral coats of a clear matte sealer.

The porcelain dolls have a wire armature inserted into them after the porcelain parts have been china painted. The dolls' bodies are then hand-sewn of cotton around the armature and filled with a special pliable material. When finished, the dolls can be repositioned numerous times.

Most of her dolls' wigs are mohair, but she uses Persian lamb's wool when it suits the doll.

Early Kwartler dolls were one-of-a-kind, using no molds. Porcelain dolls are made in limited editions of duplicates.

Once the doll is put together, its costume is researched, then carefully designed in the manner of the period being depicted. She makes a paper pattern from which to cut the clothes. In order for the garments to drape naturally, she uses the thinnest fabrics: China silk, very fine old lace, satins, cottons and woolens. Every item is a complete entity; there are no "false fronts." Each is hand-sewn. Every edge is either lined, faced, hemmed or edged so that there are no raw edges. Most vests, sweaters, jackets, coats and hats are completely removable, as is proper for these very real little beings.

Attitudes or "body language" are as important as dress. Her people relate to each other and act out little slices of life. As with larger "real people," Mrs. Kwartler's dolls are of all shapes, sizes and nationalities. They come from all walks of life, as well as from the world of literature and fantasy.

The stories the dolls tell are gentle, funny and nostalgic. There is a Victorian wedding couple who are scared stiff to go on their honeymoon because they do not know what to do. There is an encounter between a sly, self-confident delivery man and a timid, dirty-faced, shocked kitchen maid. Two children of the Victorian era are caught at the moment they meet Grandma. The boy is overjoyed; the girl draws back in fear. A little girl, *Tearful Tina,* stares in disbelief at her broken doll. Tears run down her cheeks. A daddy is caught beside the fireplace before he is quite finished putting on his *Santa* suit. *Jack Mahoney* hugs *Helga,* the hefty middle-aged cook whose cooking he loves. *Lord Armitrage* is interrupted at the bathroom sink in his long johns, his suspendered pants still unbuttoned and sagging to his knees.

In 1981, Mrs. Kwartler began her line of 2'' = 1' (5.1cm = 30.5cm) dolls which she intends also to execute in porcelain. As with her doll house dolls, these sculptures show great animation and detail. Their larger size enables her to show even more aspects of the dolls' personalities. *Red Riding Hood,* the first of this group, is found gaily tripping through the woods (pre-wolf), one of her feet in the air, her shoe in hand.

Sheila Kwartler signs and dates all of her dolls.

Sheila Kwartler is a member of the United Federation of Doll Clubs (UFDC), the Original Doll Council of America (ODACA) and the National Association of Miniature Enthusiasts (NAME).

**Illustration 9-7.** 6½in (15.5cm) *Dracula* and 5½in (16.5cm) *Dracula's Bride.* Polyform heads and lower limbs. Turning heads. Patent pending. Wire armature padded bodies. *Photo courtesy of John Noble, Museum of the City of New York.*

**Illustration 9-6.** 6in (15.2cm) *Lord Armitrage.* Polyform head and lower limbs. Padded wire armature body.

**Illustration 9-8.** 6in (15.2cm) *Sabrina.* Polyform head and lower limbs. Turning head. Patent pending. Padded wire armature body.©1979. *Photo courtesy of John Noble, Museum of the City of New York.*

**Illustration 9-9.** 5½in (14.0cm) *Liz* and 3½in (8.9cm) *Helen.* Polyform heads, lower limbs. Wire armature padded bodies.

**Illustration 9-11.** 6in (15.2cm) *Maxwell.* Polyform head, lower limbs. Wire armature padded body.

**Illustration 9-10.** 5½in (14.0cm) *Victoria* and 6in (15.2cm) *Edmund.* Polyform heads, lower limbs. Wire armature padded bodies. Mohair hair.

**Illustration 9-12.** 1½in (3.8cm) *Lolly.* All polyform. Mohair wig.

**Illustration 9-13.** 9in (22.9cm) *Little Red Riding Hood*. Polyform head and lower limbs. Wire armature cloth body. ©1981.

**Illustration 9-15.** 5½in (14.0cm) *Mlle Jou Jou de la Chambre*. Porcelain shoulder plate with swivel head, porcelain lower limbs. Wire armature. Hand-sewn fabric body stuffed with polyester fiberfill over armature. Seam between head and shoulder plate disguised by necklace. Mohair wig. ©1981.

**Illustration 9-14.** 6in (15.2cm) *Rodney* and 5½in (14.0cm) *Fawn*. Caption: "Rodney, dearest, put aside your revolver. Cyril merely stopped by to borrow a cup of sugar." Porcelain shoulder plates with swivel heads, porcelain lower limbs. Wire armature. Hand-sewn fabric body stuffed with polyester fiberfill over armature. Seam between head and shoulder plate on *Fawn* disguised by necklace. Mohair wigs. ©1981.

**Illustration 9-16.** 5½in (14.0cm) *Fawn* and *Cyril*. Caption: Fawn: "Did you see what he did?" Cyril: "Who, me?" Porcelain shoulder plate, lower limbs, swivel heads. Cyril shows wire construction in armature. Fawn has hand-sewn fabric body over armature, stuffed with polyester fiberfill. Mohair wigs. ©1981.

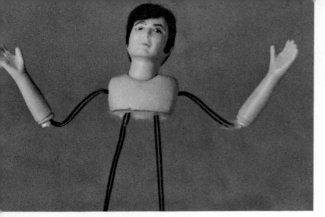

**Illustration 9-17.** Detail of Illustration 9-16, showing shoulder plate.

**Illustration 9-19.** Detail of Illustration 9-16.

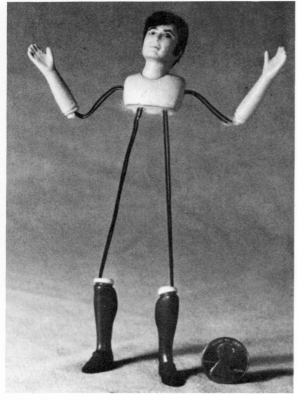

**Illustration 9-18.** Detail of Illustration 9-16, showing armature construction.

**Illustration 9-20.** 2-7/8in (7.3cm) *Penny* and *Peter.* Porcelain swivel heads and limbs. Stuffed fabric bodies over wire armatures so they can be posed. Balanced to stand by themselves. Mohair wigs. ©1981.

# 10. Anne Luree Leonard
# Porcelain, Wax

Anne Luree Leonard has been making original dolls of porcelain bisque since 1969. At that time there were very few practicing doll artists and very little information was available about porcelain work. Mrs. Leonard learned through trial and error.

After quite some time, she at last designed a 10in (25.4cm) tall portrait doll of her son, Doug E. Leonard. Portrait commissions from friends started her business rolling.

Now the California artist designs dolls in sizes from 1in (2.5cm) to 42in (121.9cm) in height and uses porcelain and wax to create them. To date (1981), she has sculpted about 30 dolls of miniature size. Most of them are one-of-a-kind. Some are limited editions. They range from 1in (2.5cm) to 9in (22.9cm) in height. At times they are 1" = 1' (2.5cm = 30.5cm) scale.

Anne Luree's dolls have either all-bisque construction or soft bodies with heads and limbs of porcelain or wax. Wax dolls always have soft bodies.

Their hair is either self-material (sculpted) or a wig of human or synthetic hair.

Most of Anne Luree's dolls are portraits, often done from photographs, although the artist also likes to do characters and "whatever happens to be in my mind at the time." This results in babies, toddlers, children, adults, historical dolls, characters from fiction and critters that are "just for fun."

Their clothes are designed and made by the artist depicting the era appropriate to the doll's concept.

Anne Luree Leonard dolls are copyrighted, signed and dated.

Anne Luree Leonard is a member of the United Federation of Doll Clubs (UFDC), the Original Doll Artist Council of America (ODACA) and the California Association of Porcelain Artists.

**Illustration 10-1.** 8in (20.3cm) *Angel* and *Elfie.* All porcelain. Jointed. Set-in eyes. Synthetic wigs.

**Illustration 10-2.** 8in (20.3cm) *Baby Devil.* All porcelain. Jointed. Set-in glass eyes. Human hair wig.

**Illustration 10-3.** 8in (20.3cm) *Angel, Elfie, Candy* and *Pete.* All porcelain. Jointed. Set-in eyes. Synthetic wigs.

**Illustration 10-4.** 4in (10.2cm) *Elf.* One-piece porcelain head, torso and lower limbs. Movable arms. Painted eyes. Molded-on painted clothing. © 1981.

**Illustration 10-5.** 3in (7.6cm) *Baby Eloise.* Porcelain head, lower limbs. Cloth body. Glass eyes. Synthetic wig.

**Illustration 10-6.** 3in (7.6cm) *Baby Eloise* and 4in (10.2cm) *Mary Jane. Baby Eloise:* porcelain head, lower limbs. Cloth body. Glass eyes. Synthetic wig. *Mary Jane:* all bisque. Jointed, molded painted hair and shoes. Hair ribbon inserted through molded-on hair loop.

Eloise        Mary Jane

**Illustration 10-7.** 3in (7.6cm) *Toddler.* All porcelain bisque. Jointed. Set-in glass eyes. Mohair wig.

**Illustration 10-8.** 3in (7.6cm) *Snow Baby.* Porcelain bisque. Painted eyes.

# 11. Erin Libby Porcelain

**Illustration 11-1.** 1" = 1' (2.5cm = 30.5cm) scale *Babette.* Porcelain bisque head, sculpted torso, lower legs and arms from the elbows down. Nylon tricot body fabric. Arms are not stuffed. The sit-upon is well padded. The thighs are lightly stuffed. Wires run from the head through the neck. Arms and legs wired for poseability. Wig is mohair on net base. © 1981.

Erin Libby has an extensive background in fine arts. She has studied, worked and exhibited in both the United States and France.

Many of Erin Libby's industrial doll designs are well-known to doll collectors. From 1966 to 1971 she worked for Mattel Toys where she was manager for doll characterization, among other things. Since 1971, she has free-lanced, working for well-known companies: Fisher-Price, Kenner, Tonka, Ansco, Shindana and others.

Together with her mother, Colleen Libby, who joined her in 1973, she is responsible for such designs as the first six Fisher Price dolls, the new *Ginny* by Vogue dolls and a burping doll for the same company, the *Snuggles* line, *Whoopsie, Pretty Curls* and a *Bandaid* doll for Ideal. *Azrak-Hamway* (Remco) has her wiggly-bodied doggy.

**Illustration 11-2.** 1" = 1' (2.5cm = 30.5cm) scale *Violetta.* Porcelain bisque head, sculpted torso, lower legs and arms from the elbows down. Nylon tricot body fabric. Arms are not stuffed. The sit-upon is well padded. The thighs are lightly stuffed. Wires run from the head through the neck. Arms and legs wired for poseability. Wig is mohair on net base. © 1981.

**Illustration 11-3.** Detail of Illustration 11-2.

In 1980, she began to work in porcelain, executing for the first time her own designs. She chose to do her first work in miniature for several reasons. She had fond memories of the small dolls she had dressed when she was young which were revived when a friend showed her some miniature dolls made from Super Sculpey and Fimo, two synthetic clays. Also, since she was a novice at working in porcelain when she designed her first dolls, the notion of finishing a large surface in that material seemed a bit intimidating.

These dolls are done in 1" = 1' (2.5cm = 30.5cm) scale, of slipcast china painted porcelain bisque. They have poseable heads, a sculpted torso, lower legs and arms from the elbow down. The body fabric is nylon tricot. The arms are not stuffed. The sit-upon is well padded. The legs (thighs) are lightly stuffed. Wires run from the head through the neck. Arms and legs are wired for poseability and hair is mohair on a net base.

Erin sees *Violetta* as "a Victorian charmer - - at home in the carriage, under a parasol or in her own bedroom, dressing. She is like a little Degas, washing her toes in a basin." (See the Introduction to this book for a discussion on Degas and his doll.)

Indeed, *Violetta* does have a very "French" air to her, like the ladies in an Impressionist painting, perhaps. But she is more abstract and simplified to the point that this is truly a miniature doll, not a real person in miniature.

Ms. Libby attributes this to her work with commercial dolls which are highly abstract. Even when they are apparently realistic, she reports, actually they are greatly simplified. This is because of the manufacturing processes for the materials from which they are made.

There is a gentle sweetness to Erin Libby's dolls. They have a languid, fragile, dreamy quality which is a bit removed from the work she has done for doll manufacturers. "Most of my work has been aimed at being lovable. The industry designs are aimed at an audience I refer to as Mrs. America. I don't mean it unkindly. It's just that when a million dolls are the sales quota, I have to feel the pulse of what almost any mother across the country is feeling."

Each Libby doll, even when made from the same mold (she makes her own molds), is different. Painting, hairstyles and clothing vary. Sometimes the torso is trimmed to a shoulder plate. The dolls are offered dressed in Victorian styles, undressed and in kits.

Erin Libby dolls are marked on the heads © ERIN LIBBY.

**Illustration 11-4.** 1" = 1' (2.5cm = 30.5cm) scale *Babette* and *Solange.* Porcelain bisque head, sculpted torso, lower legs and arms from the elbows down. Nylon tricot body fabric. Arms are not stuffed. The sit-upon is well padded. The thighs are lightly stuffed. Wires run from the head through the neck. Arms and legs wired for poseability. Wig is mohair on net base. © 1981.

# 12. Sylvia Lyons Porcelain

Sylvia Lyons' *Porcelain People* have a theatrical air. Maybe that is because their designer has for years worked part-time as a dance teacher in ballet, tap and gymnastics in Alameda, California.

There is something seriocomic in the slightly unrealistic faces of these folk which fits in well with the world of the stage. It is almost as if these beautiful beings are hiding their true emotions under a masque for the higher purpose of amusing the viewer.

And they do have style. There is a certain flair to the way they dress and position themselves. They look like they are ready to perform.

*Porcelain People* began to appear, in limited engagements, in 1975. Since then, the troupe has grown yearly in scope and number.

(Some 60 characters have come forth.) It attends doll and miniature shows from coast to coast as well as one-month performances at selected galleries in the United States.

These dolls are made from Ms. Lyons' sculptures and molds of slipcast china painted high-fire porcelain bisque. They are generally in 1″ = 1′ (2.5cm = 30.5cm) scale, although some are also 1/2″ = 1′ (1.3cm = 30.5cm) scale, and a line of "toys" is of various small sizes.

Doll house family dolls are made with porcelain heads and limbs and have cloth

**Illustration 12-1.** 6in (15.2cm) *Circus Bear.* Other bears in proportion to him. Left to right: *Little Standing Bears, Pooh-like Bear,* multi-jointed *Circus Bear,* the *Three Bears: Mama, Papa* and *Baby.* All-bisque porcelain. China painted.

bodies, but many Lyons dolls are all bisque. In 1980 a line of multi-jointed 1" = 1' (2.5cm = 30.5cm) scale all-bisque dolls and bears was introduced. These intricately engineered sculptures can take complicated positions, thanks to the combination of porcelain parts and the elastic cord which strings them together. The multi-jointed dolls include a grimaldi clown, a (white faced) mime, a harlequin-like marionette, a circus bear with a real sense of presence and *Mother 1980*. *Old Lace* is an elderly lady with a cloth middle, porcelain legs and multi-jointed upper arms and torso. A double-headed all porcelain jointed baby, about 2in (5.1cm) in size, is most unusual.

There are fairy tale characters such as *Alice in Wonderland*, *Mother Goose* and *Old King Cole*, as well as a minor coven of witches, *Charlie Chaplin*, *Santa*, a tiny French tart, a Bordello lady, a Hobbit-like person and an all porcelain pig in Ms. Lyons' menagerie.

To complete the theatrical metaphor, at times the artist designs complete environments in needlesculpture for her dolls. One of these was created for *Alice in Wonderland* and displayed at the 1977 San Diego convention of the National Association of Miniature Enthusiasts (NAME). It featured *Alice* and an all porcelain caterpillar in a multicolored soft-sculpture Wonderland, complete with enormous mushroom.

*Porcelain People* are done in limited editions. The number of the edition is usually set at the time of their design. All dolls are numbered, signed and dated.

Sylvia Lyons is a member of the United Federation of Doll Clubs (UFDC), the National Association of Miniature Enthusiasts (NAME) and the International Guild of Miniature Artisans (IGMA).

**Illustration 12-2.** 1" = 1' (2.5cm = 30.5cm) scale multi-jointed dolls: *Mime, Mother 1980, Double-headed Baby,* and *Old Lace*. Porcelain bisque strung with elastic. Mohair wigs. *Old Lace* has cloth lower torso. Mohair wig.

**Illustration 12-3.** 6in (15.2cm) Right to left: Multi-jointed *Grimaldi Clown, Circus Bear, Mime* and *Marionette*. 2½in (6.4cm) *Pig*. Porcelain bisque. Jointed with elastic and/or wire. Mohair wigs.

# 13. Suzanne Marks Porcelain

**Illustration 13-1.** 5½in (14.0cm) *Mother* and 3¼in (8.3cm) *Boy* and *Girl*. All porcelain. Fully jointed. Molded-on hair and footgear.

Suzanne Marks describes her dolls as "purely expressions of love and joy . . . influenced by children I see and adults I've known."

Her dolls have a nostalgic, warm feeling about them. Her porcelain children bring a smile to the lips. They may be actively playing dress up or attending a tea party. Perhaps they are snuggling near *Mama* for one last hug before the family portrait is taken.

The few adults to invade this child's world are invited guests, special people: *Mama,* or perhaps the mimes, *La Comédie* or *Le Tragique.*

Marks dolls are 1" = 1' (2.5cm = 30.5cm) scale, of high-fire slipcast porcelain. They have all-porcelain construction and are strung with elastic. The heads, arms and legs move.

The molded hair, skin, lips and shoes are painted with matte china paint. The eyes are done with glossy china paint. The faces, hats and legs of the mimes are glazed at the greenware stage with white underglaze - - a difficult process, as it is hard to see where one has painted.

Suzanne's early dolls were made of Sculpey, a synthetic clay, with their clothing painted on them. The miniature porcelain child dolls are dressed in hand-sewn clothing which

**Illustration 13-3.** 3½in (8.9cm) *Sue* and *Ned*. All porcelain jointed dolls with molded hair. *Sue* wears removable "Mommy's shoes" of Sculpey. Portraits of artist and her husband as children.

**Illustration 13-2.** *The Tea Party:* 3¾in (9.6cm) *Maggie* and *Jenny.* 2in (5.1cm) *Doll.* All porcelain. Fully jointed. Sculpted hair. *Maggie* has open mouth, red and white dress, black Sculpey "dress up" shoes. Feet are pointed down to fit into shoes. *Jenny* in brown dress, red hat. Red Sculpey "dress up" shoes. Feet sculpted with toes that point downward toward floor when in sitting position.

she has designed to resemble garments worn by children in the late 1800s - early 1900s.

Each doll is designed to reflect motion and/or emotion. They are all "doing something," even if it is just sitting in a chair, dangling legs over its edge, like *Maggie*, a 3¾in (9.6cm) tall toddler. *Jenny*, a 3¾in (9.6cm) little girl has feet which point down as if trying to touch the floor. *La Comédie* and *Le Tragique*, the mimes, have body stances which reflect their emotions.

Mrs. Marks makes multiples of her dolls.

Suzanne Marks dolls are stamped on the back of the torso:

SUZANNE MARKS
USA (date)
©

They are signed SM © on the back of the neck.

Suzanne Marks is a member of the Original Doll Artist Council of America (ODACA).

**Illustration 13-5.** 3¾in (9.6cm) *Annie* and *Stefan*. All porcelain bisque jointed dolls with molded, china painted hair. Molded-on footwear.

**Illustration 13-4.** 3½in (8.9cm) *Ned*. Portrait of the artist's husband as a child. All porcelain jointed doll with molded hair china painted red-blonde. Molded-on shoes and socks. Blue sailor suit. Carries lollipop made of Sculpey.

**Illustration 13-6.** 5½in (14.0cm) *Le Tragique*, Mime doll. All porcelain fully jointed doll. Face and legs glazed white in the greenware state. Dressed in navy blue suit with maroon hat trimmed in navy.

**Illustration 13-7.** Detail of Illustration 13-6.

**Illustration 13-9.** Detail of Illustration 13-8.

**Illustration 13-8.** 5½in (14.0cm) *La Comédie,* Mime doll. All porcelain. Fully jointed. Face and legs glazed white in the greenware state. Costume of maroon with navy hat.

# 14. Ellen McAdams
# Porcelain and Ceramic Bisque

"By Terri" is the name Ellen McAdams signs on her dolls. They are 1" = 1' (2.5cm = 30.5cm) scale and depict people of the second half of the 19th century: ladies of fashion, ladies of ill repute (saloon girls and bordello ladies), cowboys, a miner, brides, a corpulent gentleman in velvet smoking jacket, an oriental actress in kimono and obi, Negro servants, babies and many, many children. *Mrs. Claus* and circus figures add variety to the list.

These dolls are made of low-fire slipcast ceramic bisque or high-fire slipcast porcelain bisque from Ellen McAdams' sculptures and molds. Body construction varies. A few are all bisque. Most have bisque head and limbs with the balance of the body of cloth-covered wire armature, stuffed with sawdust. Hair is made of silk or mohair which is often curled with a hot iron.

Costumes are meticulously researched and sewn. Great care is taken to ensure that the dolls assume natural stances. Indeed, every doll is self-supporting; it can stand on its own. This adds to the realism the artist strives for.

**Illustration 14-2.** 5½in (14.0cm) *Lacey 1874.* Ceramic bisque shoulder plate, lower limbs. Cloth body with wire armature. Mohair wig. 1981.

**Illustration 14-1.** 2½in (6.4cm) *Baby Sally.* Ceramic bisque. Mohair curls. 1981.

Some dolls are limited editions. Others are open editions, discontinued when the artist tires of them.

Ellen McAdams: dolls are signed:
"by Terri"
© (date)
on the lower body, except on head and shoulder models.

Ellen McAdams is a member of the Original Doll Artist Council of America (ODACA).

**Illustration 14-3.** 4in (10.2cm) *Kirstin* and *Sailor Boy*. Ceramic bisque shoulder plates, lower limbs. Cloth bodies with wire armatures. Mohair wigs. Dressed as children of 1894. Removable footgear. 1981.

**Illustration 14-5.** 6in (15.2cm) *Albert*. Ceramic bisque shoulder plate and lower limbs. Cloth body with wire armature. Mohair wig. 1981.

**Illustration 14-4.** 5½in (14.0cm) *Lil* and *Shady Lady*. Ceramic bisque breast plates, lower limbs. Cloth bodies with wire armatures. Mohair wigs. 1981.

58

**Illustration 14-7.** 4in (10.2cm) *Susie* and *David*. Ceramic bisque shoulder plate and lower limbs. Cloth body with wire armature. Mohair wig. 1981.

**Illustration 14-6.** 5½in (14.0cm) *Victorian Lady, 1890-98.* Ceramic bisque shoulder plate and lower limbs. Cloth body with wire armature. Mohair wig. 1981.

**Illustration 14-8.** 5½in (14.0cm) *Julia,* 1890-98 (two versions). Ceramic bisque shoulder plate and lower limbs. Cloth body with wire armature. Mohair wig. 1981.

# 15. Helen McCook
# Porcelain, Cloth

Helen McCook says that her dolls are made of the strongest material there is - - love. Indeed, they are. Her gentle portraits of friends, family and strangers reflect the love and care that goes into them.

Helen works primarily in china painted high-fire slipcast porcelain bisque, but makes dolls of whatever material seems suitable. This includes cloth and auto body filler which she feels is superior to composition, readily available and unbreakable.

Many years of art training and art teaching comprise the formal background of her dolls. She once worked as a sculptor for Cybis Porcelain, an experience which helped Mrs. McCook to refine her dolls and to learn aspects of working in her chosen medium which are seldom divulged to laymen. She also paints, primarily in watercolors, specializing in genre scenes. She annually shows her work in both two and three dimensions at Christmastime in New Hope, Pennsylvania.

Through her regular articles and drawings in *The Doll Maker,* a magazine published bimonthly in Washington, New Jersey, and through doll making classes she teaches near her Pennsylvania home, she has shared her wealth of knowledge freely with others and

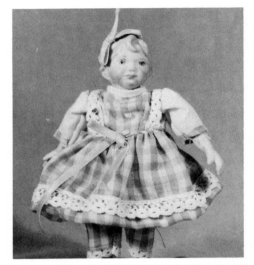

**Illustration 15-2.** 5in (12.7cm) *Sarah.* Portrait doll. Porcelain shoulder plate, lower limbs. Stuffed cloth body. Ribbon through porcelain loop in molded, china painted hair.

has helped countless doll makers to improve and perfect their work.

Mrs. McCook now makes slipcast porcelain dolls in eight sizes, starting with a portrait doll which is 18in (45.7cm) tall. By making a succession of molds from the heads which have been reduced in the firing, she brings them down to 15in (38.1cm), 9in (22.9cm), 6in (15.2cm) and doll house size, which usually is from 3in (7.6cm) to 6in (15.2cm).

The heads, arms and legs are made of porcelain. She does cast the doll house dolls in auto body filler but only upon request. In this medium they are almost indestructible and are safer for younger children. The bodies are soft. Sometimes she uses wire to make them poseable, but really prefers them soft so that they can strike doll-like poses or curl up in her hand.

She says, "I like a doll that *feels* good - - like a comfort stone - - and feel that children enjoy these more than the stiffer ones, but I do make both."

Sculpted dolls nearly all have sculpted hair, but several have mohair wigs: *Samantha, Ivy, Jenny* and *Mary* among them.

**Illustration 15-1.** 2in (5.1cm) *Breccia* and 4½in (10.2cm) *Jennifer.* Portrait dolls. The infant has porcelain head with one eye open, one eye closed, painted hair. Cloth body. *Jennifer* has porcelain shoulder plate and lower limbs, cloth body, mohair wig.

**Illustration 15-3.** 6in (15.2cm) *Joy.* Portrait doll. Porcelain shoulder plate, lower limbs. Stuffed fabric body. Mohair wig.

**Illustration 15-4.** Detail of Illustration 15-3.

She also makes a set of all-cloth tiny dolls. These she paints with acrylics. She seals their surfaces with white glue. They bend at the shoulders and hips but can be posed if wires are inserted.

Mrs. McCook's dolls are portraits of glowing, smiling children. They have a lifelike

quality to them that is uncanny in the larger sizes. In smaller size, they are charming. Often the dolls are members of her family: her children, grandchildren and ancestors. But she also does commissioned portraits. She states that she depicts the world around her.

In miniature scale, the Pennsylvania doll artist has made many one-of-a-kind portrait dolls and miniature dolls but does not have a record of them as they were done for fun and given as gifts. She did not start making dolls with the idea of making money. It was the natural creative thing to do for her. Not until 1968 did she start to make a family of dolls that would be sold as *The Peace Dolls.*

She is asked over and over what does PEACE mean in the title. She replies, "It means Peace in the mind, Peace in the home," for this is where peace begins.

Mrs. McCook has about ten original doll house doll molds. These make up into an extended doll house family: two fathers, several mothers and a group that she calls the *Tiny Playmates.* There is also a baby that is the doll house version of two infant portrait dolls which began as 18in (45.7cm) tall: those of her niece, *Kim,* and Edwina Mueller's great granddaughter, *Breccia.*

*Samantha, Mickey, Jonny, Joy, Jenny, Katie, Melissa, Sarah* and *Andrew* are 6in (15.2cm) tall and also come in the 4in to 5in (10.2cm to 12.7cm) size.

*Tiny Playmates* are 3in to 5in (7.6cm to 12.7cm) tall. Their clothing is contemporary - - the 1930s to the 1980s. The dolls

**Illustration 15-5.** 4½in (11.5cm) *Tiny Playmate.* Porcelain shoulder plate, lower limbs. Stuffed cloth body. Molded, china painted hair.

are only sold dressed. They are made in very limited editions.

There is an "M" incised in the hand of each McCook doll. Mrs. McCook explains why: "When my daughter, Mickey, was about five years old, she came running into the house one day, and excitedly showed me her new discovery - - an 'M' in the palm of each hand. 'Mommy, my initials are on my hands - - M and M - - Mickey McCook! Somebody signed me!' She was delighted and I explained to her that it was God's signature - - the signature of the Maker. 'God made you,' I said. 'That is God's mark.' Since that time, I have made it a point to look at thousands of hands and have found that we are all signed by the Maker. Some are not quite as sharp as others, but it is definitely there. We are all unique, one-of-a-kind editions of one only, fashioned by the Maker."

Helen McCook's dolls are signed with a big "M" on all of her doll heads and on each hand and foot.

Helen McCook is a member of the United Federation of Doll Clubs (UFDC), the New Hope Art League and the Buck's County Art Alliance.

**Illustration 15-6.** 6in (15.2cm) *Jonny.* Portrait doll. Porcelain shoulder plate, lower limbs. Stuffed fabric body. Molded china painted hair.

**Illustration 15-7.** Detail of Illustration 15-6.

**Illustration 15-8.** 6in (15.2cm) *Mickey.* Portrait doll. Porcelain shoulder plate, lower limbs. Stuffed fabric body. Molded hair with applied curls. Ribbons attached through porcelain curls.

**Illustration 15-9.** 4.5in (11.5cm) *Tiny Playmates.* Porcelain shoulder plates, lower limbs. Stuffed fabric bodies. Molded china painted hair. Ribbon attached through porcelain hair loop on girl.

**Illustration 15-11.** 4½in (11.5cm) *Tiny Playmate.* Porcelain shoulder plate, lower limbs. Stuffed fabric body. Molded, china painted hair.

**Illustration 15-10.** 7½in (19.1cm) *Father.* Porcelain shoulder plate, lower limbs. Stuffed fabric body. Molded, china painted hair.

**Illustration 15-12.** 4½in (11.5cm) *Tiny Playmates* with 5in (12.7cm) *Mother Katie.* Porcelain shoulder plate, lower limbs. Stuffed fabric body. Molded, china painted hair.

**Illustration 15-13.** 12in (30.5cm) *Joy* with doll house scale *Joy.* Porcelain shoulder plates, lower limbs. Stuffed fabric bodies. Large doll has human hair wig. Mohair wig on smaller doll.

**Illustration 15-14.** This illustration shows the diversity of Helen McCook's art work. A portrait in oil, *Mickey* is displayed beside porcelain doll, *Mary Rose.* From 1978 Christmas-time Bank Show in Pennsylvania.

**Illustration 15-15.** Larger McCook dolls and water color painting at December, 1978, Bank Show held in New Hope, Pennsylvania.

# 16. Irma Park Porcelain

**Illustration 16-1.** 2in (5.1cm) *Katie* holds a 7/8in (2.2cm) *Doll.* 1-7/8in (4.7cm) *Fisher Boy.* Wax-coated china painted porcelain bisque heads and limbs. Bodies have wrapped wire base. Hair of combed yarn.

Irma Park's dolls capture the diversity of childhood days from 1776 to the 1920s. Her children are happy, sober, smiling and are almost always engaged in a typical childhood activity.

The dolls are meticulously dressed and accessorized. The little girls and boys often hold dolls, hoops, teddy bears, and so forth, as they stand on their bases. None of them is larger than 2in (5.1cm) tall.

Miss Park works in high-fire porcelain bisque. The large dolls, those over 1-1/8in (2.8cm) in height, have heads, arms and legs of high-fire porcelain bisque that is china painted and then coated with wax. The small ones which begin at 1/4in (0.65cm) have only heads made of waxed porcelain and wrapped arms and legs. The bodies are on a wire base and wrapped. Some of the dolls that are 1in (2.5cm) and under have painted hair. Others have hair of combed yarn.

Since 1966, the California artist has specialized in depicting children, dolls' dolls and various characters and babies. Among the 1in (2.5cm) tall characters are: *Li'lest Peddler,* with tray and trinkets, *Tom Thumb,* leprechaun, clowns, *Madonna,* rabbits, mice and *Little Rags.* Babies range from 5/8in

(1.6cm) to 1¾in (4.5cm) tall. Dolls' dolls are from 1/4in (0.65cm) to 2in (5.1cm) in height. The children, finally, are from 1-3/8in (3.4cm) to 2in (5.1cm) tall.

When Miss Park began making dolls, they were much larger than her present work. One of her earlier efforts was 5ft (1.5m) tall and made of cloth. Late in 1963, she created her first 2¾in (7.1cm) miniature adults, working out her techniques over months via trial and error. Her *Notion Grannie* was sold through Kimport Dolls in 1964. Other characters of the same size followed, and soon Miss Park was in business.

Working in such a minute scale is difficult. Miss Park explains, "The little dolls are very tedious and every step time consuming to make. Being a lover of detail, I sometimes add too much on a new addition to the line, without thought of how wearisome it will be making duplicate after duplicate. Or even with the sample, battle with a toy or detail I know will continue to give me trouble. And although added to the list, it is with a hope that only a few orders will be placed on that certain doll. It is those with extra detail and ones that

**Illustration 16-2.** 1in (2.5cm) *Convention Visitor* and 1-7/8in (4.7cm) *All Dressed Up* with 11/16in (1.8cm) *Doll.* Wax-coated china painted porcelain head, wrapped wire bodies. Large doll has porcelain limbs also. Combed yarn hair.

**Illustration 16-3.** 2in (5.1cm) *Betsy,* a two-face doll, and 1-7/8in *Ellie* hold 1in (2.5cm) *Dolls.* Turn *Betsy's* head and she smiles. Also turn back the skirt and reverse her doll, to reveal a head that is not broken. Wax-coated, china painted porcelain bisque heads and limbs. Wrapped wire bodies on large dolls. Small dolls have same construction, without porcelain limbs. Combed yarn wigs.

give trouble in the making that come up discontinued sooner or later. I work with a tray on my lap, seated on a couch with work tables by my side. Often times one of the tiny dolls will slip from my fingers and fall to the floor, and the 'old lady' is down on her knees searching.''

Since 1966, Miss Park has made about 36 different children on bases and close to 100 other dolls. The number made of each doll varies from one-of-a-kind to over 159 duplicates. Difficulty of execution and popularity of design determine the production.

The certification and label reproduced below are glued to the back clothing of every Irma Park doll - - from the 1/4in (0.65cm) to the 2in (5.1cm) ones. They are in two sizes, depending on the space available for placement. "IRMA PARK" is a registered trademark.

Irma Park is a member of the United Federation of Doll Clubs (UFDC), the National Institute of American Doll Artists (NIADA) and the National Association of Miniature Enthusiasts (NAME).

**Illustration 16-5.** 1-5/8in (6.8cm) *Broken Doll* No. 2, with a 1in (2.5cm) *Doll,* 1-7/8in (4.7cm) *Christmas Stocking.* Wax-coated, china painted porcelain bisque heads. Wrapped wire bodies. Combed yarn wigs.

**Illustration 16-4.** 1-1/8in (2.8cm) *Chubby,* 1in (2.5cm) *Clown,* 1in (2.5cm) *Li'lest Peddler.* Wax-coated, china painted porcelain bisque heads. Wrapped wire bodies. Combed yarn wigs.

# 17. Jan Riggs
# Porcelain

Jan Riggs' dolls have an unusual body construction for their small size. They follow the time-honored tradition of combining porcelain heads and limbs with a jointed leather body. This is difficult to execute in a scale of 1″ = 1′ (2.5cm = 30.5cm).

The soft leather body is stuffed with sawdust. The dolls are jointed at the knees, hips, shoulders, elbows and wrists. They have swivel heads. Their wigs are of mohair.

Mrs. Riggs, who has worked with porcelain and china painting for many years and has painted portraits for several galleries, has made original dolls since 1977 and is self-taught. Her dolls are one-of-a-kind or made in small editions (no more than five of any one). They are supple and poseable, not wire-bodied, because the artist likes people to actually play with her work.

The California doll maker aims at realism and usually devises a vignette for each doll to interact with which heightens the character chosen for it. Each doll, thus, becomes a small three-dimensional genre painting which may be repositioned by its owner.

She specializes in depicting children from different eras and especially likes to make Indian children as they really appeared in the 19th century. Women dressed in fashions from various eras are also popular. Historical figures, cowboys, boys, even Dracula are members of her cast of characters.

Mrs. Riggs is particularly careful with her costuming. Each garment is carefully

**Illustration 17-1.** 3in (7.6cm) *Girl with French Fashion Body.* Porcelain shoulder plate with swivel head, porcelain limbs. Jointed leather body stuffed with sawdust. Mohair hair. Glass eyes.

researched to be authentic for the period it portrays and is meticulously executed to add the finishing touch to each doll. Whenever possible, laces, braids and other ornaments are handmade to be accurately scaled to the

**Illustration 17-2.** 6in (15.2cm) *Cowboy.* Porcelain head and lower limbs. Jointed leather body, mohair wig. Glass eyes. Body stuffed with sawdust.

size of the doll. She does not exclusively use antique materials for costuming, but considers it a challenge to be able to use contemporary fabrics and make them fall naturally into place without having to glue or sew the folds into place. Because she makes the dolls jointed, she feels the dress should move with the dolls.

Riggs dolls are only sold fully dressed and in vignettes.

Jan Riggs dolls are signed on the shoulder plate: J.R. 19-- no.-- © in china paint. "Jan Riggs" is signed in longhand also. A NIADA certificate mark is stamped onto the leather body.

Jan Riggs is a member of the United Federation of Doll Clubs (UFDC), the National Institute of American Doll Artists (NIADA) and the National Association of Miniature Enthusiasts (NAME).

*Jan Riggs* 19— ©

**Illustration 17-3.** 6in (15.2cm) *Cowboy.* Porcelain head and lower limbs, jointed leather body, mohair wig. Glass eyes.

**Illustration 17-4.** 5½in (14.0cm) *Mermaid.* Porcelain upper body, fabric lower body, mohair hair, set-in eyes. 1978.

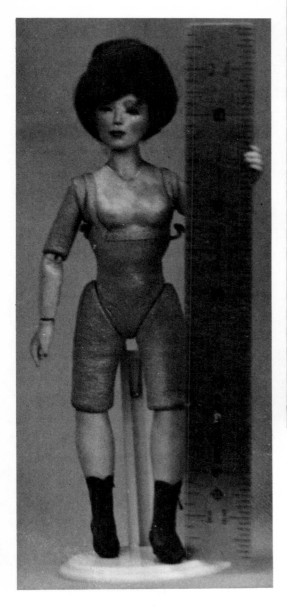

**Illustration 17-6.** 4in (10.2cm) *Melinda sewing.* Porcelain head, lower arms and legs. Leather body. Fully jointed. Mohair hair.

**Illustration 17-5.** 5¾in (14.7cm) *Gibson Girl.* China painted porcelain head, torso, lower arms and legs with molded-on shoes. Leather torso, upper arms and legs. Fully jointed. Mohair wig. Illustration shows original body construction.

# 18. Marty Saunders Porcelain

Illustration 18-1. 1" = 1' (2.5cm = 30.5cm) scale *Figure from Portrait by J. S. Copley, 1765.* China painted porcelain shoulder head with molded hair, lower limbs. Wire armatured fabric body.

Marty Saunders recreates American history in miniature. She sculpts one-of-a-kind portrait dolls in high-fire porcelain bisque. Her subject matter is Americans of the past and present, both famous and unknown.

She began doll making at the age of three when she remade the doll her mother had lovingly dressed for her. Even then she had an image of what she wanted her dolls to look like. "I've been trying to reach that goal ever since," she says.

Mrs. Saunders spent much of her childhood in the artists' colony of Santa Fe, New Mexico.

Illustration 18-2. 1" = 1' (2.5cm = 30.5cm) scale portrait of *Rose* from the television series, "Upstairs, Downstairs." China painted porcelain shoulder head with molded hair, lower limbs. Wire armatured fabric body.

Art was a way of life there. She absorbed its influence early and learned, informally and formally, to work in many media. As she grew older, her interests broadened to include a love of history and costume. These, combined with her talent for portraiture, formed a reservoir of skills tailor-made for the creation of original dolls.

In 1975, she succumbed to requests of a neighbor, Betty Valentine, who creates furniture in miniature scale, and agreed to make a special doll for her in porcelain, a new medium for the Massachusetts artist.

After making inquiries, she decided against making slipcast dolls, as the technique displeased her. So she just started sculpting the porcelain. "It was love at first handful," she reports. Finally, she had a material with which she could create the dolls she had dreamt of years before.

She made, perhaps, 20 dolls that first year. Most of them were undressed as Mrs. Saunders was in love with the sculpting. Then she saw that the customers who bought her work had different ideas than she about how the dolls should be dressed. She just had to have control of them, so she learned to dress them as well.

"Now I knew why I had been studying old costumes all my life. My love of history, art, costume, sculpture, portraiture and porcelains all culminated in these little figures. Sculpting portraits of people in miniature was more fun than painting their portraits," she recounts.

Using historic portraits (her knowledge of art history comes in handy here), or photographs - - antique or contemporary, or old fashion plates, Mrs. Saunders sculpts likenesses of Americans, capturing the essences of their personalities in as many aspects as she can. When she is doing a portrait of someone, she tries to find out as much about his life and lifestyle as possible.

Her dolls are meticulously planned as to color scheme and attitude from the outset. She starts each doll by drawing her ideas on paper. Each one is completely sketched, both body and costume: underwear, outerwear, even the shoes are rendered. "I am very careful to dress the dolls in the correct fabrics, styles and colors for the periods to be depicted," Mrs. Saunders notes.

To do so, she picks out fabrics, laces and trims from her large collection of rare silks, cottons, wools and laces. With the fabrics in a Ziploc bag and the drawings beside her, she begins to sculpt the doll's head and limbs. She makes a dozen dolls at a time, sculpting their heads and limbs directly in high-fire porcelain. Shoes are sculpted also in porcelain, and each doll must have the correct shoe for its period.

When one works directly in a water-based clay like porcelain, he has to let it rest a bit between sessions with the sculpting tool. Working on 12 heads at a time enables the artist to work continually without wasting time waiting for her clay to respond properly to her. "I make a dozen dolls at a time," she says, "because I can start and continue to work solidly for three days on 24 hands. Any more or any less would leave me odd hours of work. The hands are the most tedious work, and the heads are the most fun. Head making days are the best days of the month."

The Massachusetts woman enjoys the challenge of working in porcelain and seeing how far she can push the medium. Dolls are china painted, after the porcelain firing, to heighten the portraiture and complement the fabrics used. As each doll is painted, the artist can refer to her fabrics which she has at hand in the Ziploc bags and match their colors.

When the dolls have been china fired, a special flexible wire is inserted into the limbs and epoxied into place. This makes the dolls poseable. A cotton fabric body is made to

**Illustration 18-3.** 5in (12.1cm) *1871 Ladies Chatting.* China painted porcelain shoulder heads, lower limbs. Wire armatured fabric bodies.

**Illustration 18-4.** Rear and front views of Illustration 18-3.

cover the wire armature, and the head is then glued into place. The dolls are then dressed. Each costume is hand-sewn with the greatest of care. Nothing is glued. All seams are finished so that the underside of the doll is pleasing.

Marty Saunders works in several scales. Her best-known work is 1" = 1' (2.5cm = 30.5cm) scale. But she enjoys the change of pace of 1/2" = 1' (1.3cm = 30.5cm), 3/4in =

**Illustration 18-5.** 6in (15.2cm) *Turn-of-the-century Gentleman* and 4½in (11.5cm) *Boy.* China painted porcelain shoulder heads with molded hair, porcelain lower limbs. Wire armatured fabric bodies.

**Illustration 18-6.** 4in (10.2cm) *1871 Girl.* China painted porcelain shoulder head with molded hair, porcelain lower limbs. Wire armatured fabric body.

1' (2.0cm = 30.5cm) and 1½" = 1' (3.8cm = 30.5cm) scales. Her largest work is in 2" = 1' (5.1cm = 30.5cm) scale size. These figures appeal to the doll collector rather than to the miniaturist, and the costuming detail can be much more precise. Moreover, the clothes can be removable in this size without interfering with the realistic illusion. The closings are sewn down on the garments of the smaller figures.

Marty has made about 600 miniature dolls and almost all of them have been one-of-a-kind. On rare occasions she has made two dolls alike, although individually sculpted, so that two family members may have portraits of a person. Once in a while she makes a limited edition of six dolls of a famous person. In that case, again, each doll is separately modeled.

Dolls' subject matter ranges from Americans of the 1600s to the portraits of her son and his bride that were fabricated for the top of their wedding cake. She has made portraits of black people and a Pueblo Indian and is dying for a customer who had a lovely oriental grandma.

One of the dolls Mrs. Saunders most enjoyed making was for an elderly lady who had worked on her doll house for years and did not want to leave it when she died. Marty made a doll of her at her most beautiful age, so she could be forever young in the dream house.

Marty Saunders' dolls have been exhibited alongside her paintings at her one-woman shows. They are also on exhibit at a number of historical societies and museums, a fitting tribute to their accuracy of depiction and their sculptural qualities.

Marty Saunders dolls are marked on the chest plate with a letter indicating to her the scale, the doll, a number indicating the order

**Illustration 18-7.** Detail of Illustration 18-6.

of the making of that head that year (each year the numbers are started over), a mark that indicates she made the doll and the year the doll is made. Sometimes she also adds the year the figure depicts.

A sample marking might be: A (1''=1'), 15 (number of that head) Ⓢ her mark and 81 (the year the head was made).

A name tag is sewn into the clothing of the doll that has Mrs. Saunders name, the same numbers and the copyright mark.

Marty Saunders is a member of the United Federation of Doll Clubs (UFDC), Doll Study Club of Boston and the National Association of Miniature Enthusiasts (NAME).

**Illustration 18-9.** 1'' = 1' (2.5cm = 30.5cm) scale *Portrait of Betty Morgan's Grandmother.* Porcelain shoulder plate with molded hair, porcelain lower limbs. Wire armatured fabric body.

**Illustration 18-8.** 1'' = 1' (2.5cm = 30.5cm) scale *Portrait of Baby.* China painted shoulder head with molded hair, porcelain lower limbs. Wire armatured fabric body.

**Illustration 18-10.** 3/4'' = 1' (2.0cm = 30.5cm) scale *1900 Lady.* Porcelain shoulder plate with molded hair, porcelain lower limbs. Wire armatured fabric body.

**Illustration 18-11.** Approximately 1½in (3.8cm). *Dollhouse doll's doll.* One of a kind porcelain bisque. China painted. © 1980.

# 19. *Annie Shickell Porcelain*

Annie Shickell learned to do ceramics as a child working at her mother's side. She worked her way up to porcelain reproductions of antique dolls and graduated to making originals in slipcast porcelain bisque in April 1977. Along the way, she was encouraged in her work by NIADA artists Helen Kish and Faith Wick.

Her dolls are primarily in 1" = 1' (2.5cm = 30.5cm), and she prefers working small. "I have tried a few larger dolls," she says, "but my loves are miniature. I have even dreamt in mini, like opening your lunchbox or your desk when you are only five years old and finding this whole new, tiny world inside when everything around you is bigger than you are!"

Shickell porcelain dolls primarily have cloth-covered wire armature bodies so that they "mind," but some are all bisque also. Their original sculptures are in Sculpey, and the artist makes her own plaster molds from them. They range in size from tiny dolls' dolls to 7½in (19.1cm) tall. Some of the dolls have sculpted hair, others mohair wigs. Mrs. Shickell buys white mohair and experiments with different colors and dyes. "Sometimes you do

**Illustration 19-1.** 6in (15.2cm) *Fred* and *Murphy.* China painted porcelain shoulder plates, lower arms and legs. Wire armatured fabric bodies. Molded-on shoes with "real laces." Limited editions of 50 each.

**Illustration 19-2.** 4.6in (16.8cm) *Anne* (self-portrait of artist as a child) and *Daniel* (portrait of artist's son). China painted porcelain shoulder plates, lower arms and legs. Wire armatured fabric bodies. Mohair wigs. Limited editions of 50.

Illustration 19-3. 5in (12.7cm) *Sarah.* China painted all porcelain doll with mohair wig. Gold-tone metal neck and ankle bracelets. Limited edition of 50. *Margory Hoya Novak Collection.*

Illustration 19-4. 5in (12.7cm) *Andrew.* China painted porcelain shoulder plate with molded hair, porcelain lower legs and arms. Molded-on boots with "real" laces. 5in (12.7cm) *Sarah.* China painted all porcelain doll with mohair wig. Gold-tone metal neck and ankle bracelets. Limited edition of 50.

Illustration 19-5. 7½in (19.1cm) *Mrs. C.* holding 2in (5.1cm) *Doll. Mrs. C.* has china painted porcelain shoulder plate, hands and shoes. Fabric body. Mohair wig. All porcelain small doll.

come out with unusual colors this way, but others come out more natural than the standard colors offered by supply houses . . . If anyone is interested in green, maroon or purple mohair, please write!" she says.

The artist prefers to make "sculpted shoes that really appear to have a foot in them." At the same time she likes real laces, bows, gold buckles, and so forth, and her dolls' footgear combines to two. There may be "real" shoelaces on sculpted boots, as is the case with her miniature artist.

Mrs. Shickell's dolls are realistic little people. Some of them are portraits, as is the case with *Annie,* a 4.6in (11.5cm) self-portrait of the artist as a child, or *Daniel,* a 4.6in (11.5cm) portrait of her son. Others are done for comedy effect, such as the 5.11in (12.8cm) clown baseball players, *Fred* and *Murphy.* Still others are fantasy people, such as 4½in (11.5cm) *Norward,* the Guardian of the Northern Gate.

A combination of realism and gentle satire is *"Mrs. C.,"* a 7½in (19.1cm) turn-of-the-century doll collector who won first prize and the Judges' Choice award at the Table Mountain Treasures Doll Show in Denver, Colorado, (March 1980). This elderly lady is posed squinting through a lorgnette at a small porcelain doll, also by Mrs. Shickell, which she holds in her hand. She is no doubt ascertaining its quality.

Perhaps the most challenging of the dolls is 5in (12.7cm) all-bisque *Sarah,* the nude model who is laying on her side posing for an artist. To achieve this effect without the creation of a jointed doll, it was necessary to saw the original sculpture into several parts and cast it in pieces. Immediately after the greenware has set up, it is removed from the

**Illustration 19-6.** 4½in (11.5cm) *Norward, Guardian of the Northern Gate.* China painted porcelain shoulder plate, lower limbs. Wire armature. Cloth body. Mohair wig. Limited edition of 100.

Annie Shickell is a member of the United Federation of Doll Clubs (UFDC) and the Original Doll Artist Council of America (ODACA).

**Illustration 19-7.** 6.2in (15.5cm) *Elias* and 5.6in (14.2cm) *Marette.* China painted porcelain bisque shoulder plates, lower limbs. Wire armature. Fabric bodies. Mohair wigs. Limited editions of 50 each.

mold and rejoined, using porcelain slip as a glue. This tricky procedure enables the figure to have its difficult undercuts which permit a realistic positioning of limbs.

In addition to the limited editions (50 or less dolls), Annie Shickell also does one-of-a-kind dolls, but she hates to part with these.

Dolls are available in kits or bodied and fully dressed. The Colorado doll maker designs their costumes but has two seamstresses who help with the sewing. She, however, does all the finishing touches and makes the dolls' props.

Annie Shickell dolls are marked on the back of the head or on the shoulder plate back:
i.e.  #1/50          #1/50 KIT
      ©1980          ©1980
      Annie Shickell  Annie Shickell
Dolls also bear a pink arm tag reading: "Original by Annie." The above information is within the tag.

**Illustration 19-8.** 7½in (19.1cm) *Beth* holding green package. China painted porcelain bisque shoulder plate, lower limbs. Wire armature. Fabric body. Mohair wig.

# 20. Jeanne Singer
# Porcelain

**Illustration 20-1.** 6in (15.2cm) *Father,* 5-7/8in (14.9cm) *Mother* and 2in (5.1cm) *Infant. Father* and *Mother* have porcelain bisque breast plates and lower limbs, molded shoes, china painted molded hair. Cloth bodies over wire armatures, intaglio eyes. *Infant* is all porcelain, has swivel head and movable limbs, china painted. ©1980.

Jeanne Singer's designs in slipcast high-fire porcelain bisque have an uncanny naturalism.

Their designer's early art training was in pottery, sculpture and costume design. After her marriage, she designed porcelain flowers for Vee Jackson and designed statuary for Victory Ceramics, both in Pasadena, California.

While her family was growing, she became a full-time housewife and mother, feeding her aesthetic needs with art courses including oil portrait painting, tailoring, drafting and building design.

**Illustration 20-2.** Detail of Illustration 20-1. Note particularly the intaglio eyes which have holes in them to indicate the pupils.

In 1971, she began carving apple dolls. By the mid 1970s she expanded her doll making materials to burlap and bread dough. She also made statuary and perfected her mold-making skills.

When, in 1977, she was introduced to antique porcelain dolls, she already had the skills necessary for the creation of her own porcelain dolls.

Her first work included the *Year of the Child* dolls, a group of lifelike ethnic children which she exhibited at the 1979 convention of the United Federation of Doll Clubs which was held in New York City. These won her four ribbons.

Other designs include a life-size porcelain baby and a fashion model dressed in an "ERTÉ" style silk dress.

Miniature Singer dolls include a 4in (10.2cm) tall infant in a christening dress and three 5in (12.7cm) porcelain and cloth babies. These realistic infants represent children of three races: caucasian, black and native American. The features and color of each doll are

**Illustration 20-3.** 3½in (8.9cm) *Little Girls* and 2in (5.1cm) *Infant.* Two girl dolls are all porcelain with movable arms and legs, molded-on shoes. Seated girl has swivel head and mohair wig. Standing girl has stationary head, painted hair. Baby is all porcelain, fully jointed. All ©1980.

**Illustration 20-5.** 6in (15.2cm) *Grandfather* and 5½in (14.0cm) *Grandmother.* China painted porcelain breast plates, lower limbs. Molded hair, molded shoes. Cloth bodies over wire armatures. ©1980.

**Illustration 20-4.** *Doll house family:* 6in (15.2cm) *Father,* 5½in (14.0cm) *Grandmother,* 5-7/8in (14.9cm) *Mother,* 6in (15.2cm) *Grandfather.* Front row: 3½in (8.9cm) *Little Girls,* 2in (15.1cm) *Baby.* All ©1980.

appropriate. They have porcelain heads and limbs and are bendable at hips, waist, elbows and shoulders.

The Singer doll house family is a modern one consisting of parents, grandparents, a little girl and a baby. They are done two ways. Some have stationary heads with molded hair. Others have swivel neck heads and mohair wigs. Adult dolls have porcelain heads, upper bodies, lower legs and arms. They are on a wire armature and bend at knees, elbows and hips, waist and shoulders.

The little girl doll is all porcelain and jointed. The all porcelain baby has a swivel neck.

The doll house family is dressed convincingly in clothing of the period of one's choice. The modern family wears contemporary styles and fibers, something seldom achieved successfully by doll artists because of the technical problems of draping synthetic fabrics on such small dolls.

Most Singer dolls are multiples, original designs reproduced with a mold. Mrs. Singer has made at least one directly-modeled composition doll house family and intends to experiment in wax.

The 5in (12.7cm) baby is signed either with a "J.S." or a "J. Singer" at the back of the neck.

Doll house dolls with swivel necks are signed at the back of the neck, "J.S."

One-piece head and breast plate dolls are signed "J. Singer" on their backs.

Jeanne Singer is a member of the United Federation of Doll Clubs (UFDC) and the Original Doll Artist Council of America (ODACA).

**Illustration 20-6.** 5in (12.7cm) *Caucasian Infant.* Porcelain head and limbs. Cloth body. Bendable at hips, waist, elbows and shoulders. ©1980.

**Illustration 20-7.** 5in (12.7cm) *Black Infant.* Porcelain head and limbs. Bendable at hips, waist, elbows and shoulders. ©1980.

# 21. Sarah Sorci

**Illustration 21-1.** 6in (15.2cm) *1900 Male Doll* and 5in (12.7cm) *1900 Female Doll*. Male: Head and torso to waist are molded porcelain. White shirt and blue tie are molded porcelain bisque. Molded brown hair, blue eyes. Arms and legs (with molded-on shoes) of porcelain bisque. Cloth body with armature. Wears navy blue suit. Female: Porcelain head and torso to waist, porcelain lower limbs, molded-on shoes. Cloth body. Hair is a combination of human and synthetic hair pulled back in a pink ribbon. Dress of fine white batiste material with lace and pink satin belt. ©1980. These two dolls won first place ribbon at IDMA competitive exhibit in Phoenix, Arizona, 1980.

Sarah Sorci was born into an artistic family. From a very young age artistic activities were a way of life, but she never considered this to be anything special. She had a natural flair for sculpting and drawing and particularly enjoyed drawing the human figure. Her talent was recognized in sixth grade and she was encouraged in this vein through high school, but she never received formal training.

It was not until she had been married 14 years and was looking for an artistic outlet that she fell back on her early inclinations and began to make dolls. This was in 1960.

Her first three dolls were portraits of Stalin, Churchill and Roosevelt, and they began their lives as clay busts. A friend suggested that Sarah make them into dolls.

As she knew nothing about ceramic processes, all had to be learned. Working in low-fire ceramics displeased her, and she was at the point of giving up when she discovered porcelain. She has been working exclusively in this medium ever since.

Mrs. Sorci's dolls are made of slipcast high-fire white porcelain bisque. The flesh tones and other coloring are china painted and fired onto the porcelain. No precolored porcelain is used.

Mrs. Sorci makes the complete doll from the original clay sculpture and molds through the wigs and clothing. Her dolls range in size from 18in (45.7cm) to doll house. The latter are in 1" = 1' (2.5cm = 30.5cm) scale.

Their bodies are a combination of porcelain and cloth-covered wire. They are porcelain

**Illustration 21-2.** 5½in (14.0cm) *High Fashion Model*. Porcelain head and torso to waist. Porcelain lower limbs. Molded-on shoes. Balance of body of cloth. High fashion hairdo made of combination of human and synthetic hair. Blonde hair, blue eyes. Red satin dress with black metallic lace over it. © 1980.

to the waist and have porcelain limbs. The lower body, upper arms and upper legs are wire covered with cotton and cloth to make them bend to different positions. Their hair is either molded in the porcelain or wigs that are a combination of human and synthetic hair.

These little people are generally dressed in contemporary fashions. As these are time-consuming, costumes are rarely duplicated. The women, men and children are high-fashion models who display the diversity of the fashions of the 1980s, and they are represented as engaging in activities of the 1980s. The high fashion ladies are taller than the normal doll house women Sarah Sorci makes. They stand 5¾in (14.7cm) tall, as compared to 5in (12.7cm) or 5½in (14.0cm).

Dolls representing contemporary grand-parents, blacks and other ethnic groups are also in the Arizona doll artist's miniature population.

All Sorci dolls are limited editions repro-duced from her molds and available only fully dressed.

Sarah Sorci dolls are marked:

$$S_{ORCI}^{ARAH} © 1980$$

Sarah Sorci is a member of the United Federation of Doll Clubs (UFDC), the Original Doll Artist Council of America (ODACA), the International Doll Makers Association (IDMA) and the Western Porcelain Portrait Artists Association (WPPAA).

**Illustration 21-3.** 5½in (14.0cm) *High Fashion Model.* China painted porcelain head and torso to waist. Porcelain lower limbs. Molded-on shoes china painted yellow. Balance of body is cloth. Brown human hair, brown china painted eyes. Yellow handkerchief linen dress with yellow satin ribbon belt and adornments.

**Illustration 21-4.** 5½in (14.0cm) *High Fashion Model.* China painted porcelain bisque head and torso to waist. Porcelain lower limbs. Molded-on porcelain western boots china painted brown. Balance of body is cloth. Hair is wig made of combination of human and synthetic hair. Wears blue jeans with white stitch-ing on front and back pockets. Western plaid shirt (blue, red and yellow). © 1980.

**Illustration 21-5.** 5½in (14.0cm) *High Fashion Model.* China painted porcelain bisque head and torso to waist. Porcelain lower limbs. Molded-on china painted shoes. Balance of body of cloth. Black wig made of combination of human and synthetic hair. Brown china painted eyes. Wears navy blue check polyester knit hand-sewn jump suit.    © 1980.

**Illustration 21-6.** 5½in (14.0cm) *High Fashion Model.* China painted porcelain bisque head and torso to waist. Porcelain lower limbs. Molded-on china painted shoes. Balance of body of cloth. Blonde wig made of combination of human and synthetic hair. Blue china painted eyes. Wears teal blue silk dress with tiny flower print, lined in polyester.    © 1980.

**Illustration 21-7.** 5¾in (14.7cm) *High Fashion Models.* China painted porcelain bisque heads and torsos to waists. Porcelain lower limbs. Molded-on china painted shoes. Balance of bodies cloth. Left doll: brown hair wig, brown china painted eyes. Wears light green handkerchief linen dress, green china painted shoes. Middle doll: dress is pink hem-stitched silk organza. Matching belt. Elastic inserted in sleeves at wrists. Back opening has three handmade button holes. Buttons are pink seed beads. Pink china painted shoes. Right doll: dress is voile material with black background and tiny red, pink, yellow and green roses. Red silk belt. Elastic inserted in sleeve at the wrists. Black t-strap shoes. All three dolls have wigs made of human and synthetic hair.

# 22. Deidra Spann Porcelain

All photographs courtesy of Deidra B. Spann

**Illustration 22-1.** Deidra B. Spann, doll artist.

Deidra Spann is a designer/artist born and raised in Washington, D.C. Her undergraduate and graduate training in art was at the Howard University, Department of Fine Art. Her favorite media were batik, welded sculpture, inlaid wood, ceramics and textile design. Intricacy and delicacy in combination with bold design were her trademarks.

After graduation, she worked in several different capacities in the art field but became bored with each of them after a short time, because they only utilized one medium of expression. She felt unchallenged and under-utilized aesthetically.

It was then, in the spring of 1974, that dolls came into her life via her mother, who "dragged" her to a doll making class. Although the techniques taught were comparatively primitive, the artist discovered a field of expression in which she could use all her talents, and, incidentally, be her own boss.

She studied the market and learned everything she could about doll making in preparation for creating her own dolls in porcelain. In the meantime, she made dip 'n' drape craft dolls which sold well but were only a stopgap

**Illustration 22-2.** 4¾in (12.2cm) *Little Victorian Girl.* Front view. China-painted porcelain bisque head, arms and legs. Bendable body with wrapped insulated copper wire armature. Mohair wig. All-silk and 100% cotton fabric. Signed: db SPANN '80.

until she had the opportunity for porcelain work. Mrs. Spann credits this market research for her early success in doll making.

Deidra Spann's dolls are mainly in 1" = 1' (2.5cm = 30.5cm) scale. She began working in porcelain on this scale because it seemed to be a perfect size for learning techniques and because of the challenge involved in designing small bodies and garments. Her larger dolls are 15in (38.1cm) to 18in (45.7cm) tall, but they are not numerous.

The bodies of the miniature dolls are of an insulated wire doubled and wrapped with a fabric paper to be in proportion. They are then painted with a flexible glue to ensure a longer life. The head and limbs are porcelain bisque and are glued on with epoxy for durability.

**Illustration 22-3.** 4¾in (12.2cm) *Little Victorian Girl.* Back view of Illustration 22-2.

**Illustration 22-4.** 4¾in (12.2cm) *Little Victorian Girl.* Close-up of Illustration 22-2.

Their designer tries to construct each doll so that it can be passed on for generations. They are by no means delicate except that the porcelain is breakable, and they stand on their own with a bit of sticky wax under the feet.

The wigs are made of curly mohair and are fabricated directly on the head. For the men and some of the women the artist uses Persian lamb. At times a man's hair will be painted on.

Spann is very meticulous in the dressing of her dolls and goes to great pains to make

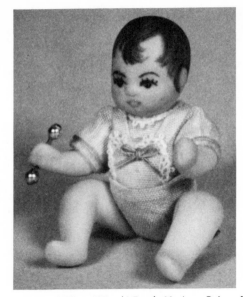

**Illustration 22-5.** 1¾in (4.5cm) *Modern Baby.* All porcelain. Painted hair. Broadcloth fabric. Sterling silver rattle.  © 1980.

them realistic. Her advice to the dresser of miniature dolls is the following: "The main thing I say when I talk to people about making miniature dolls is, first and above all, think TINY and not small when it comes to choosing trims and fabrics. Don't settle for what you think will look cute. Make sure that everything is scaled down and not too thick, heavy or wide. Just the slightest offset detail can mean the difference between your doll looking like a doll or looking like a little person. The major mistake I see people making is that they don't realize that the waistline MUST be small to start with, especially if the clothing is going to be bulky or there's going to be a wide flared skirt. Whittle away at that fabric as though you were tailoring it for real."

Her dolls are dressed in colonial, contemporary and Victorian clothes. Dolls are dressed in garb from 1910, 1920 or the 1940s, contemporary people from various nations in their native clothing, and also as historical and well-known figures.

She has plans to capture the feeling of African dancers and ballet dancers in motion but in doll form. That is why she came up with the name "Doll Sculptures." "The kinds of dolls that I wanted to make were very realistic, but I felt that some may become so much so that they would lean towards being sculpture but not really fit in that category, either," the artist confirmed in an interview.

Deidra Spann dolls are done in multiples, except perhaps for their clothing. Some are one-of-a-kind. At least 20 different dolls have

**Illustration 22-8.** 6in (15.2cm) *Modern Black Man.* Back view. China painted porcelain bisque head, arms and legs. Bendable body with wrapped insulated wire armature. Special type of yarn for hair. Cotton and knit fabric. Real leather trim. Signed: db SPANN '80.

**Illustration 22-6.** 5½in (14.0cm) *1909 Era Lady.* Back view. China-painted porcelain bisque head, arms and legs. Bendable body with wrapped insulated copper wire armature mohair wig. Dress of 100% silk fabric. 100% cotton slip and pantalets. Straw hat with silk ribbons. Tiny black beads sewn on back for buttons. Signed on shoe bottom: db SPANN '81.

**Illustration 22-9.** 6in (15.2cm) *Modern Black Man.* Front view of Illustration 22-8.

been designed. They are made in kits, undressed or dressed.

Deidra Spann dolls are signed on the bottom of the shoe: d.b. (year), SPANN is incised on babies usually on the underside of right leg. They carry her tag reproduced below.

Deidra Spann is a member of the National Association of Miniature Enthusiasts (NAME).

**Illustration 22-7.** 5½in (14.0cm) *1909 Era Lady.* Front view of Illustration 22-6.

ayanna
doll sculptures

deidra b. spann/designer

**Illustration 22-10.** 6in (15.2cm) *Modern Black Man.* Close up of Illustration 22-9.

**Illustration 22-13.** 5-1/8in (13.0cm) *Colonial Woman.* 5½in (14.0cm) *Colonial Man.* China painted porcelain bisque shoulder plates, arms and legs. Bendable bodies with wrapped insulated copper wire armatures. Dressed in 100% silk. Woman has fine sterling silver headband around hair. Mohair wigs, gold thread buttons. Signed: db SPANN '80.

**Illustration 22-11.** 1¾in (4.5cm), undressed measurement. *Little Black Baby.* Front view. All porcelain bisque. China painted. Jointed with wires. Sterling silver rattle.

**Illustration 22-14.** 4¾in (12.2cm) *Little Colonial Girl.* China painted porcelain bisque shoulder plate, arms and legs. Bendable body with wrapped insulated copper wire armature. Mohair wig. All-cotton fabric. Silk bow. Signed: db SPANN '81 on bottom of shoe.

**Illustration 22-12.** 1¾in (4.5cm) *Little Black Baby.* Back view.

Illustration 22-15. 4¾in (12.2cm) *Little Colonial Girl.* Close up of Illustration 22-14.

Illustration 22-17. 5½in (14.0cm) *Victorian Lady.* China painted porcelain bisque shoulder plate, arms and legs. Bendable body with wrapped insulated copper wire armature. Mohair wig. 100% cotton dress fabric. Silk belt and bow. Cotton slip and pantalets. Signed: db SPANN '80 on shoe.

Illustration 22-16. 5¾in (14.7cm) *Victorian Man.* China painted porcelain bisque shoulder plate, arms and legs. Bendable body with wrapped insulated copper wire armature. Persian lamb wig. 100% wool fabric. Cotton shirt. Signed: db SPANN '80 on shoe.

Illustration 22-18. 5½in (14.0cm) *Victorian Lady.* Detail of Illustration 22-17.

# 23. Eunice Tuttle Porcelain

Eunice Tuttle has succeeded in capturing the past and reanimating it in miniature. She depicts children with such startling naturalism that it is difficult to ascertain from a photograph their size or substance. Their size is small. She works in 1″ = 1′ (2.5cm = 30.5cm) scale. Their substance is porcelain.

The New Jersey artist sculpts children who range in age from infancy to 16 years and in size from 2½in (6.4cm) to 5in (12.7cm).

These little people are, more often than not, recreations of real children of the past. She finds their images in paintings (famous and not) and photographs and strives to reproduce them faithfully in clay. This she does with remarkable verisimilitude. The student of art history can recognize many of her subjects with ease: Goya's *Don Manuel Osorio* (The Boy in Red), Renoir's *Girl with a Watering Can*, Velazquez' *Infantas*, Sargent's *Children of Edward Boit*, *Little Miss Hatch* and the baby from the painting "The Hatch Family" by Eastman Johnson, and a portrait of her niece, Ellen Mary Cassatt, by the American Impressionist painter, Mary Cassatt.

**Illustration 23-2.** 4in (10.2cm) *Ellen Mary Cassatt in 1896.* All porcelain bisque fully jointed one-of-a-kind doll. Wig made of rayon soutache braid. Taken from the painting of her at age two, by her aunt Mary Cassatt. 1979 Christmas card.

There are Kate Greenaway children and children as limned by unknown American folk artists. Memory and reality are also tapped. Miss Tuttle has made portraits of herself, her brothers and her mother from old photographs. She also sculpts contemporary children, both black and white.

Childhood favorites such as *Buster Brown* (and his dog, Tige) and *Mary Jane* are also in Miss Tuttle's repertoire.

This talented lady began working in porcelain as an offshoot of the exigencies of her teaching job. In 1942 it became necessary for her to teach ceramics in her art classes in the White Plains, New York, public schools.

**Illustration 23-1.** 1″ = 1′ (2.5cm = 30.5cm) scale *Self-Portrait at Age of Five Years with my Doll and Carriage.* All porcelain bisque. Fully jointed one-of-a-kind doll. Wig made of rayon soutache braid. 1977 Christmas card.

**Illustration 23-3.** 4in (10.2cm) *Liz.* All porcelain bisque fully jointed doll. Wears white dress and hat, trimmed with red. © 1970.

As she knew nothing of the subject, she took a two year New York University extension course in ceramics at the County Center in White Plains. Somewhere along the line she learned slip casting, a basic procedure in making porcelain dolls.

Mrs. Amy Voorhees of the Inwood Potteries of New York was the New York University instructor. When Miss Tuttle decided that she would like to try her hand at making a doll in this, to her, a new medium, Mrs. Voorhees commissioned her to make a 10in (25.4cm) Victorian lady for the 15th anniversary dinner of the New York Ceramic Society. The head, hands and feet were of pottery clay and were done from Miss Tuttle's original model. She made the casts herself. The body of the doll, arms and legs were of old white kid gloves, and she was dressed in the style of 1892 - - a complete outfit from the skin out.

The schoolteacher was bitten by the doll making bug in a most decisive way. She acquired a small Amaco test kiln so she could do her own firing at home. Her next dolls were modeled after the style of the 4in (10.2cm) doll house dolls of her childhood, but less of the chubby little "Hausfrau" type and more like a little boy or girl of today.

She discovered, in 1953, that porcelain clay had become available to the amateur and that she could have her little kiln rewired for high-fire so that she could make her dolls in the more durable porcelain. She began making doll house dolls with a purpose. These early porcelain dolls were not scaled 1'' = 1' (2.5cm = 30.5cm). She soon found out that doll house dolls should be that size, so her earlier casts

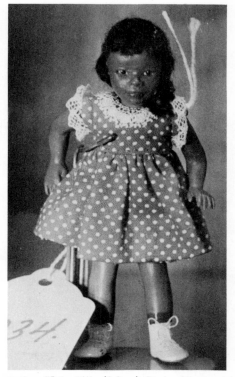

**Illustration 23-4.** 3½in (8.9cm) *Cindy.* All porcelain. Fully jointed. Wears red dress with white dots, red socks, white baby shoes. © 1964. Photograph taken at 1979 auction of items from the Margaret Woodbury Strong Museum held in New Hampshire. *Cindy* was lot No. 1034.

**Illustration 23-5.** 3½in (8.9cm) *Cindy* and *Chucky.* All porcelain. Fully jointed. *Cindy* wears red dress with white dots, red painted socks, white baby shoes with laces. *Chucky* wears red shirt with white dots, white shorts, red painted socks, white shoes with laces. © 1964.

**Illustration 23-6.** 1" = 1' (2.5cm = 30.5cm) scale *Kate Greenaway 5-Year-Old.* One-of-a-kind all porcelain jointed doll. Rayon soutache hair. © 1978.

far superior to that of mohair or human hair for such small dolls. They have a pleasing gloss. They can be set and curled with no trouble. The rayon holds a curl and can be combed and brushed like hair.

The costuming of Tuttle dolls requires much research, especially for the historical dolls and those taken from famous paintings. Even the undergarments are historically correct. Every doll can be completely undressed and redressed.

Miss Tuttle intends her figures to be DOLLS which can be played with by a child if the owner sees fit to try it. They fit well in any doll house or miniature setting and stand by means of metal pegged stands which fit into holes which extend up into the dolls' legs from the heel.

For a time, Miss Tuttle made multiples of her work, anywhere from two to sixteen of a design, but she grew tired of duplicating and reverted to just one doll of a kind. Not even sample dolls are made. She has kept no dolls of her own, with one exception - - the four-month-old *Angel Baby.* She made 105 of them and retained the first in the series for sentiment's sake.

It has become a custom for the artist to design a special doll or group of dolls each Christmas to be used for her Christmas card. This takes precedence over all else and is started in early July so that it will be ready for her to photograph in color for the card. She has standing orders for the Christmas doll - - sight unseen.

**Illustration 23-7.** 5¼in (13.0cm) *Melissa* and 2in (5.1cm) *Baby: Little Miss Hatch and the baby sister from the painting, "The Hatch Family," by Eastman Johnson (detail).* All porcelain one-of-a-kind dolls. Jointed. 1978 Christmas card.

were abandoned and in 1963, ten years after beginning to make all porcelain dolls, she settled on the 1" = 1' (2.5cm = 30.5cm) scale for good.

The dolls are slipcast with Bell's White Orchid Dark Pink porcelain into plaster casts the artist makes from her own sculptures. These have proven very durable over years of use. The cast for Miss Tuttle's *Angel Baby* has been used over 100 times and is still in excellent condition, despite its age and use.

Any differences in type or build needed for her dolls are achieved by adding or subtracting clay as needed after removing the greenware from the cast. She has standard sets of casts for the baby, a three-year-old, a five-year-old and an eight-year-old. Converting for the in-between ages, the artist says, is very simple.

The hair is always a wig made from rayon soutache braid or rayon shoelaces raveled out and, if necessary, dyed after the raveling. The actual wig is made before raveling. The proportions of wigs made from this material are

**Illustration 23-8.** 1" = 1' (2.5cm = 30.5cm) scale doll house dolls: *My Mother and her two Brothers in 1879.* (*Nelly:* 7 years, *Harry:* 8 years, *Willie:* 4 years). One-of-a-kind jointed porcelain dolls with rayon soutache hair. 1974 Chirstmas card.

Eunice Tuttle does no advertising, has no stock on hand and sells her dolls privately, through a mailing list of interested collectors. Needless to say, she sells everything she makes. "I love making the dolls but keep none of them," she states. "The sooner they are on their way to the new owners the better."

Eunice Tuttle dolls are marked with her name and the date incised on the back of the body section - - if there is room. She sometimes puts the name of the doll, itself, i.e., *Angel Baby* or *Lucie,* but that is usually not possible in the smaller dolls.

**Illustration 23-9.** 1" = 1' (2.5cm = 30.5cm) scale *Buster Brown, Mary Jane* (6-year-olds) and *Tige.* One-of-a-kind special order jointed porcelain dolls with rayon soutache hair. © 1979.

# 24. Beverly Walter Porcelain

**Illustration 24-1.** 5¾in (14.9cm) *Father Christmas.* Bisque shoulder head, bisque forearms and boots, mohair wig with exposed crown of head, mohair eyebrows and beard, veined hands. Dressed by Betty Rawls in red wool coat and hat with dark grey French knots simulating Persian lamb trim. Tree and sack by Beverly Walter.

Difficult circumstances seemed to inspire Beverly Walter to experiment with doll making. In 1970 her brother was confined to a body cast for many months. He was flat on his back and needed much mental stimulation. To provide this the siblings carved apple dolls together, making all sorts of characters complete with accessories such as *Mr. Toad, Friar Tuck, Frankenstein, Aunt Jemima* and scores of seafaring men. These were sold and the duo graduated to an oven-hardening clay, making from it such dolls as *Bruce Cassidy* and the *Sundance Kid.*

When her brother recovered, she found she was hooked on doll making but no longer had a collaborator.

In her search for a more durable material to continue her efforts, Beverly purchased a small enameling kiln which enabled her to fire dolls she sculpted and poured in a ceramic material. When these swivel-necked dolls were successful, she switched to a high-fire porcelain kiln and learned all she could about the medium, beginning with reproductions of antique dolls.

After much urging on the part of customers, she reduced the antique dolls to miniature size by means of a series of molds. She set for herself very high standards and strove to duplicate exactly the fine painting and body work of the original antiques, even in minute size.

Her first doll was reduced from 33in (83.8cm) to 5¾in (14.7cm) by making eight or so successive plaster molds, with great care to preserve each detail. When the last mold produced a "sweet young thing" in microscopic size, Ms. Walter was sold on miniatures.

The doll received a real cork pate, a tiny wig coiffed with tiny needles, beaded earrings in her pierced ears and a kid body that exactly

**Illustration 24-2.** 5½in (14.0cm) *Hannah.* Elderly lady with bisque shoulder head, veined bisque hands, bisque legs with painted molded boots. Mohair wig. Glass eyes. Cloth body. Dressed by Betty Rawls.

duplicated that of the antique F.G. Fashion Doll.

This doll was such a success that Ms. Walter began to reduce other antique dolls, to try to redo them in increasingly difficult scales and still retain the illusion of the originals.

These miniaturization experiments were conducted in the midst of the chaos concommitant to the production of original souvenir dolls for two conventions of the United Federation of Doll Clubs.

The first of these dolls was a *Scarlett O'Hara* "pincushion doll," or half-doll (that is, the head, torso and arms are of porcelain and the body is a large soft pincushion-type structure). This doll was made for the 1976 convention of the Dogwood Doll and Toy Club of Richmond, Virginia. The second doll was the enormously popular souvenir doll of the August 1980, annual UFDC Convention, held in Washington, D.C. This doll, *Father Christmas,* was begun in 1977. Fourteen hundred duplicates of it were made by Ms. Walter.

"It may seem strange," she says, "to have diverted from this enormous task at such a busy time. However, the creation of so many of one thing stifles one's creativity and, finding myself so stifled, I was, without realizing it, mentally challenging myself to find some worthy diversion and one that would not take up too much kiln space."

She soon graduated from antique reproductions to original miniature designs of her own. But she kept the quality as exacting as ever. In this she was guided, instructed and critically evaluated by her father, now deceased, the internationally known sculptor, artist and historian, Randy Steffan. In 1976, he received the George Washington Exemplar Award at Valley Forge, Pennsylvania, for having made outstanding contributions to American history through his sculptures, paintings and writings.

The dolls are sculpted in modeling clay or in porcelain clay, and then a plaster mold is made for duplicating the doll in slipcast porcelain bisque. They are then poured in blue-white porcelain slip. The artist found out early in her career that she did not care to use precolored porcelain as this did not give the lovely skin tone found in the antique dolls. This meant using only blue-white porcelain and applying all skin color.

Finding just the right firing temperature for each color was a long procedure but worth the trouble. She found out that she needed to fire skin, lashes, brows and lips separately and at different temperatures - - and in that order.

**Illustration 24-3.** 5½in (14.0cm) *Godey Lady.* Bisque shoulder head, applied hair and flowers, bisque arms and legs. Painted shoes. Cloth body. Dressed by Betty Rawls. Trunk an original by Jeffrey Breza.

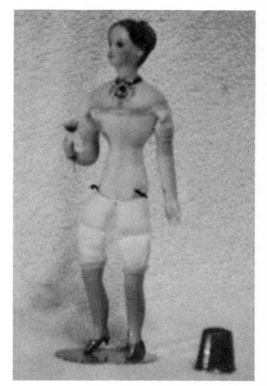

**Illustration 24-4.** 5½in (14.0cm) *Godey Lady.* Bisque shoulder head, applied comb, applied necklace with set-in stone, bisque arms and legs with painted shoes. Cloth body.

Hair is either applied and fired or mohair. The eyes are either painted or set-in glass. Bodies are constructed of cloth. Bisque or china arms are attached to them.

In 1981, Beverly Walter had completed 14 different original miniature dolls. Eight are *Godey's Ladies,* inspired by 19th century Godey fashion prints. These dolls are 5½in (14.0cm) tall, have intaglio eyes and applied hair. Each hairstyle is made individually of

**Illustration 24-5.** 5½in (14.0cm) *Godey Ladies.* Bisque shoulder head, applied hair and combs. Applied necklaces with set-in stones. Bisque arms and legs (with painted shoes). Cloth body. Dressed by Betty Rawls.

**Illustration 24-6.** Detail of Illustration 24-5, *Godey Ladies.*

thread draped onto the wet porcelain head and coated with porcelain slip. All hair ornaments, flowers, combs, ribbons, and so forth are individually formed and applied before firing.

The dolls' jewelry is applied in the wet-clay stage. Some has set-in stones. The dolls have pierced ears. Their arms and legs are bisque, and their shoes are painted with applied ornaments.

These dolls are made in bisque (unglazed porcelain) and china (glazed porcelain).

The painting of the *Godey Ladies* is very time-consuming and inspired by the techniques used on Meissen porcelains and on fine Dressel-Kester ladies. Each doll has striated eyebrows, upper and lower lashes and each hair on the head is painted separately.

*Father Christmas* (not the same as the 1980 National UFDC convention souvenir) is 5¾in (14.7cm) tall with bisque forearms and boots. He has a shoulder head and wears a mohair wig with an exposed crown of head, and has mohair eyebrows and beard. His bisque hands are veined, and he wears black boots. He has intaglio eyes and a cloth body.

*St. Nicholas* is plumper and more jovial and has intaglio eyes, veined hands of bisque and bisque boots. His hair and beard are mohair, his body is cloth. *Michael* and *Molly* are 3½in (8.9cm) twins with molded hair, intaglio eyes and bisque arms and legs with painted boots and cloth bodies. They are children of 1880 and are about three years old.

*Hannah,* an elderly lady, was originally done in 22in (55.9cm) size and has been reduced to 5¼in (13.4cm). Her hair is grey mohair; her eyes are glass, and she has veined hands and black bisque boots.

*Victoria* is an infant only a few weeks old. She has painted eyes and just a few wisps of painted hair. Her arms and legs are bisque, and her body is cloth.

Beverly Walter's dolls are dressed on special order by Betty Rawls of Virginia. Their costuming is meticulously done and complements perfectly the porcelain work.

The artist incises all her dolls on the back of the head with her name and the year. They are usually stamped in the center of the back with "B.W."

Beverly Walter is a member of the United Federation of Doll Clubs (UFDC) and the National Association of Miniature Enthusiasts (NAME).

**Illustration 24-7.** 3½in (8.9cm) *Michael.* Molded hair, intaglio eyes, bisque arms and legs, soft body.

# 25. Carol-Lynn Rössel Waugh
# Porcelain, Latex Composition

**Illustration 25-1.** 3in (7.6cm) *Baby Bear.* China painted pale yellow porcelain bisque five-piece body with movable limbs. Molded-on bottle, bow, booties, shirt. Limited edition. Signed: CWaugh. © 1980.

Books, dolls and art, these have always been my favorite things. I make little jointed dolls and, especially, little bears, of porcelain bisque or latex composition. These were not always my media. My early work was in cloth. I made a series of play dolls for children that were approximately 24in (61.0cm) tall and had winsome expressions. The best known of the group was the first doll I designed, *Nosalie.* She has become my mascot, and I have made her and her family in porcelain. In 1973 I discovered porcelain at a doll convention, read about it, then picked people's brains and experimented.

I sculpt my work, generally, in plastilina, make plaster molds and slipcast my dolls.

Sometimes I will make successive reduction molds of a design I want to make in several sizes. I then cast the bears or dolls in either porcelain or latex composition. As each shrinks approximately 20 percent as it is either fired or cured, the sizes of the figures are approximately the same.

By training I am an art historian. I have M.A. and B.A. degrees in the history of art, but my art training is negligible. Like everyone else, my work went/goes through stages. Early dolls were "biggies." But bigness and porcelain tend to be mutually exclusive for me. The timely purchase of a doll house in 1975 set me on a much better scale, as I attempted to populate it. Now my biggest dolls are about 6in (15.2cm) tall.

**Illustration 25-2.** 6in (15.2cm) *Cedric, the English Bear.* China painted pale yellow porcelain bisque. Molded-on shoes with spats have two buttons on them. Five-piece body with movable limbs. Signed on back CWaugh © 1980. "Cedric" inscribed on each shoe bottom. Knitted bear suits by H. Hunemorder, bear couturière extraordinaire. Limited edition. Also done in latex composition.

**Illustration 25-3.** 6in (15.2cm) *Cedric.* Close up of china painting and face detail of bears in Illustration 25-2. Bears shown undressed (bare) and in jogging suit.

**Illustration 25-4.** 6in (15.2cm) *Black Nosalie, Noodles* and 1½in (3.8cm) *Nosalie's Dolly.* Large dolls are china painted porcelain bisque with five-piece jointed bodies strung with elastic. Molded hair. Removable clothing. Small doll is one-piece construction with mohair wig, china painted features and shoes. ©1977. Closed editions.

Early Waugh sculpted dolls were attempts at realism. I finally discovered that this was not my strong suit. These early dolls had wire armature cloth bodies with porcelain limbs and shoulder plate porcelain heads. I hated

making the bodies. I am also not very fond of repeatedly sewing tiny clothes. This is strange, because I began making dolls by dressing my squadron of *Ginny* dolls back in the 1950s.

I did a lot of 1″ = 1′ (2.5cm = 30.5cm) doll house people: fathers, mothers, grandparents and children. Of those, the Jimmy Carter family (*Jimmy, Amy* and *Rosalynn*) was best-known, and perhaps my most realistic. *Amy* even had porcelain sneakers molded onto her feet.

Waugh dolls, circa 1980s, are of five-piece construction: one-piece torso and head, and four limbs. They are either slipcast high-fire porcelain bisque or cast latex composition. Porcelain dolls are china painted; latex ones have latex paint and are sealed for permanence. They are strung with elastic for mobility. Many of them have their clothes sculpted right on them, reminiscent of the old all-bisque dolls. But they can still wear clothes over top of the molded-on garments. The combination of the two types of garb makes for interesting texture combinations. They are balanced so they can pretty much sit and stand on their own.

I also make little one-piece "penny dolls," which are modern versions of the tiny dolls I bought in the 5 and 10 cent store when I was

**Illustration 25-5.** 5½in (14.0cm) *Googin* and *Pookin.* China painted all porcelain bisque five-piece construction. Strung with elastic. Molded hair, eyebrows, shirts, pants, shoes, socks. Names of dolls inscribed on bottom of each shoe. Dolls balanced to stand on their own. Signed: CWaugh ☉ 1981 on back of torsos. *Pookin* has removable pleated red skirt, also red shoes, red trimmings, yellow shorts. *Googin* has blue shorts, blue and red shoes. Limited editions.

**Illustration 25-6.** 2½in (6.4cm) *Baby Goo,* 1in (2.5cm) *Goldilocks, Daddy Bear, Mama Bear,* and 3/4in (2.0cm) *Baby Bear.* China painted porcelain bisque. *Baby Goo* has five-piece all porcelain body with molded-on booties, china painted socks. Balanced to stand on his own. Four small dolls have one-piece porcelain bodies with china painted molded-on hair and clothes. All © 1976. Closed editions.

small. They all have molded-on clothes and are usually holding an object and/or doing something.

My work is now seldom in 1'' = 1' (2.5cm = 30.5cm) scale. For five years, from 1975 to 1980, I worked in this size. My dolls are now more abstract, rounder and fatter and easier to dress.

Bears are my specialty, especially character bears. I find them more companionable than people dolls. I am an avid arctophile (bear lover); I collect bears and I am a member of the Good Bears of the World.

Although my work is done in "editions," they are not very big. I dislike repeating myself

**Illustration 25-8.** 3in (7.6cm) *Donut Boy.* One-piece porcelain bisque "Penny Doll" with molded-on china painted blonde hair, blue eyes, blue jeans, red sweat shirt, brown shoes, chocolate brown donut. White glass of milk. Signed on back: CWaugh © 1981. Doll is portrait of Eric-Jon Waugh at age 2½. Limited edition.

**Illustration 25-7.** 6in (15.2cm) *Jimmy Carter* and 4½in (14.0cm) *Amy Carter.* Porcelain bisque shoulder plates, lower limbs, molded shoes. *Amy* has molded-on blue sneakers. *Jimmy* has molded hair. *Amy* has mohair wig, wire glasses. Wire armatured stuffed fabric bodies. *Jimmy* wears 1976 Presidential campaign button. Jimmy © 1975. Amy © 1977. Closed editions.

and about a dozen of anything, unless it is somebody I really like, is all I can tolerate. Also, I am allergic to porcelain. More and more I will be working in latex composition. The casting processes are similar and composition produces nearly unbreakable bears. Latex composition, for me, seems too crude for miniature dolls. Bears, however, are meant to be rugged, I rationalize.

I want my dolls and bears to be played with, preferably by children. My work has no great aesthetic message. I hope it brings smiles to its viewers. Dolls are, after all, meant to be fun.

Each Waugh critter is signed on the back: "CWaugh" (in longhand) © (date). Sometimes the doll's name is also added. Earlier dolls had my name, C.WAUGH, or CAROL-LYNN WAUGH, in block letters instead of the signature, reproduced below:

*CWaugh*

I am a member of the United Federation of Doll Clubs (UFDC), the Original Doll Artist Council of America (ODACA), the Good Bears of the World, the Maine Association for Women in the Fine and Performing Arts (MAWFPA) and the Society of Children's Book Writers (SCBW).

**Illustration 25-9.** 2½in (6.4cm) *Flower Girl.* One-piece porcelain bisque "penny" doll with molded-on china painted auburn hair with bow in it, dress of pastel shade, shoes painted brown, and bouquet. Signed on back: CWaugh © 1981. Limited edition.

**Illustration 25-11.** 5½in (14.0cm) *Bearishnikova.* Light yellow china painted porcelain bisque. Five-piece construction. Jointed with elastic to dance "on point" and do various high kicks and splits. Molded-on ballet suit with flowers. Molded-on flowers in hair. Molded-on toe shoes. Signed: CWaugh © 1980 on back torso. Limited edition. Also made in latex composition.

**Illustration 25-12.** Detail of Illustration 25-11, *Bearishnikova.*

**Illustration 25-10.** 4¼in (10.5cm) *Bearlock, the Super Sleuth.* China painted all-bisque bear. Has five-piece construction. Strung with elastic. Honey-gold color. Has molded collar at neck. Hole in each paw holds "clues" or magnifying glass. Wears deer stalker cap. Balanced to stand alone. Signed: CWaugh © 1979.

**Illustration 25-13.** 6in (15.2cm) *Bearishnikov.* White porcelain bisque painted brown on head and arms. Pastel shades leotard and ballet shoes. White legs and top of ballet costume. Five-piece body construction, strung with elastic. Signed on torso: CWaugh © 1981. Also made in latex composition. Limited edition.

**Illustration 25-14.** 3in (7.6cm) *Bedtime Girl* and 2½in (6.4cm) *Bedtime Boy.* Porcelain bisque one-piece "penny" dolls. China painted molded-on clothes. Girl has nightgown with collar and cuffs, a doll in one hand which trails behind her and a bedtime book in the other. Brown painted hair and eyes. Boy has molded-on footed pajamas with "drop seat" with buttons on it. One hand holds a copy of "My Friend Bear" book, the other holds bear's hand in back. Both dolls are signed: CWaugh © 1981.

**Illustration 25-16.** 8½in (21.6cm) *Karin.* Porcelain bisque china painted head and hands. Painted-on brown hair. Brown eyes. Cloth, sawdust-filled body. Swivel neck. Wears baby cap trimmed with lace, white top with print yoke and dark solid-color pants, white socks, diaper.

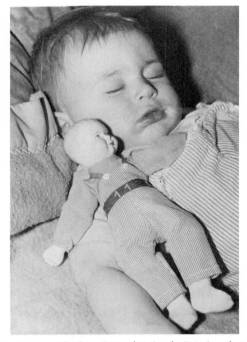

**Illustration 25-15.** 8½in (21.6cm) *Eric-Jon* (with Eric-Jon Waugh at nine months, who modeled for the doll). Porcelain bisque china painted head and hands. Molded-on blonde hair, blue eyes. Cloth, sawdust-filled body. Swivel neck on doll. Wears striped "crawlers" and jersey turtle-necked top. White socks and diaper. © 1979.

**Illustration 25-17.** Carol-Lynn Rössel Waugh. Photo taken November 1980. *Photo by Reynald Pinard,* ELBEUF, FRANCE.

# 26. Gary and Phyllis Wright Porcelain

**Illustration 26-1.** 5in (12.7cm) *Gary* by Phyllis Wright. China painted porcelain bisque head, lower limbs. Balance of body stuffed cloth. Wears pastel footed sleeper with "gripper snappers." © 1981.

Phyllis and Gary Wright form an unusual doll making duo. A mother and son team, their work is sold under the aegis of the House of Wright. Although the dolls are at times complementary, each Wright has distinct artistic interests which s/he pursues.

Phyllis, the founder of the firm, started art formally at Blackstone College in Virginia, where she majored in fine arts, and at Pratt Institute in Brooklyn, where she studied commercial art. In 1948, she began to use her training as an assistant to the display director of B. Altman & Company. Here she came in contact with many valuable art materials and experiences not generally available. Sculpting, layout, painting and drafting were skills she honed on the job that would later be useful for doll making.

After marriage in 1951, these talents submerged as she raised her sons, who inherited her interest in art. As they grew, they encouraged her to return to the art field. In 1962, she did so and for seven years taught art at Harbor Country Day School in St. James, New York. At the same time she founded Harrison-Wright

Handicrafters, which designed and made a variety of giftware items. When her partner retired for health reasons, Phyllis changed the company's name to the House of Wright and concentrated on the teaching of arts and crafts.

In 1974, however, she was hospitalized for a worsening back condition and was forced to find another outlet for her creative urges. As she was already interested in dolls, she decided to design and make her own originals of porcelain.

In 1975, the first Phyllis Wright limited edition originals were issued: a series of pert, small all-bisque children in charming "yesterday" clothing. Their winsome expressions, particularly their eyes, which are not unlike those of their creator, won the hearts of collectors. Each dolls, even if in a limited edition series, was always re-sculpted in the greenware state and painted just a bit differently so that no two dolls were ever identical.

**Illustration 26-2.** 5½in (14.0cm) *Female circa 1840s-1880s* by Phyllis Wright, 6in (15.2cm) *U.S. Navy Lieutenant - - Undress Blues, 1852-1862* by Gary Wright. Porcelain shoulder plates, lower limbs, molded shoes on feet. Kid leather bodies. Mohair wig on female. Molded moustache on male.

Illustration 26-3. 6in (15.2cm) *Male 1800-1820* by Gary Wright and 5in (12.7cm) *Female 1800-1820* by Phyllis Wright. Porcelain bisque china painted shoulder plates, lower arms, legs. Molded footwear. Mohair wigs.

Illustration 26-4. 6in (15.2cm) *Lieutenant, U.S. Navy 1852-1862 - - Summer Uniform* (white) and *First Lieutenant, U.S. Dragoon Undress Uniform, 1840-1851* (blue) by Gary Wright. Porcelain shoulder plates, lower limbs, molded-on shoes. Kid bodies, mohair wigs.

Phyllis' dolls have changed in size and scope since then. She now makes larger child-dolls, some with soft bodies, and a series of leather bodied lady dolls that are approximately 12in (30.5cm) in height.

In 1977, she and her son, Gary, began production of their line of doll house dolls. These dolls vary in their construction. Some, the babies, are all bisque. Others have kid bodies hand-sewn over a wire armature. This procedure makes it possible to position them in natural poses. These dolls are equipped with porcelain shoulder plates and lower limbs. All doll house figures have mohair wigs with the exception of the infant. Some of the men can be had with molded hair on request. The doll house population includes adult men (young-mature), adult women (young-mature), young boy (8-14), young girl (8-12), toddler child, girl and boy (2-5) and an all-bisque baby with movable arms and legs. The adult men measure 6in (15.2cm) in height. Women vary from 5¼in (13.4cm) to 5¾in (14.7cm).

The dolls are sold either undressed or dressed, representing time periods between 1750 and the early 20th century.

In 1981, Phyllis began a series of infants which are approximately 4in (10.2cm) tall. Most appropriately, the first of these is a portrait of her son, Gary.

Gary Wright's doll making is a result of his love for history, genealogy and art. In 1967,

Illustration 26-5. 5½in (14.0cm) *Lady in Corset circa 1880s* by Phyllis Wright. Porcelain china painted shoulder plate, lower limbs. Kid leather body. Mohair wig.

**Illustration 26-6.** 6in (15.2cm) *U.S. Army First Lieutenant, Infantry, 1840-1851* (right) and *U.S. Corps of Engineers Captain 1840-1851* (dark blue), by Gary Wright. Porcelain shoulder plates, lower limbs, kid leather bodies.

**Illustration 26-7.** 2in (5.1cm) *Infant* by Phyllis Wright. China painted all porcelain fully-jointed dolls. Mohair wigs.

he received a photograph of his great-great-grandfather, Henry Magrath, taken during the American Civil War when he was Captain of Company G, Twelfth New York State Militia, in 1863.

This started him on a genealogical treasure hunt, as he traced his ancestors back to the early American colonies. History came alive for him, and he began collecting early American artifacts, making miniature models of those he could not afford. It logically followed that he should create figures to interact with them.

Gary's first figures were entirely made of earthenware clay. With his mother's help, he made his first porcelain men when he was 14 years old. The soldiers were modified in construction over the years. Gradually, they included leather, metal, polyform and cloth in their makeup. Early figures had rigid poses. Today, they are of similar construction to his

mother's dolls, made in similar sizes, and have leather bodies.

All of Gary Wright's men are dressed meticulously in historically correct costumes and uniforms. A great deal of research goes into the proper depiction of not only uniforms but regalia and accoutrements. Some of his figures are portraits of famous people. *Lincoln, Admiral Dewey, Robert E. Lee* and *Stonewall Jackson* are among them. A long list of Wright ancestors, beginning with *Clement Briggs* who landed with the second ship at Plymouth, Massachussetts, in November 1621, to contemporary members of the clan is also taking tangible form. The portraits are sensitive and lifelike and have found quite a following among collectors.

Gary's dolls are commonly done in sizes to accompany lady and child dolls made by his mother: 12in (30.5cm) (approximately) or doll house size (approximately 6in [15.2cm]) tall. The doll house men have appropriate hair styles and whiskers and appropriate molded-on footwear for the time periods they represent. At present there are seven different doll house man heads to choose from. The men's military dress provides a pleasing foil for the softness of the woman dolls' garb.

Gary and Phyllis Wright are members of the United Federation of Doll Clubs (UFDC) and the Original Doll Artist Council of America (ODACA). Phyllis Wright is past president of ODACA.

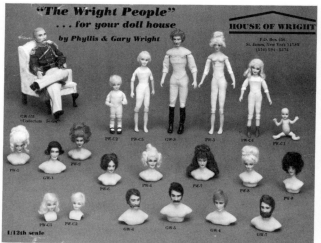

**Illustration 26-8.** *The Wright People.* Overall view of Gary and Phyllis Wright's 1'' = 1' (2.5cm = 30.5cm) scale doll house dolls. Porcelain bisque heads, lower arms/hands, and lower legs/feet. Bodies are hand-sewn kid over a wire armature. All figures have mohair wigs with the exception of the infant. No. GW-5M in upper left corner has molded hair.

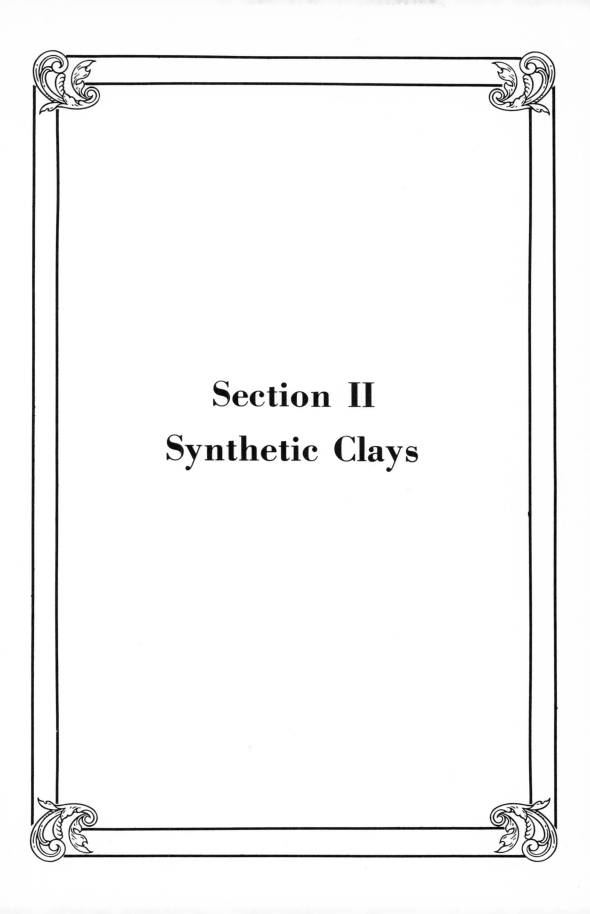

# Section II
# Synthetic Clays

Synthetic clays are relatively new on the market. They are usually petroleum-based and can be "fired," or baked, at relatively low heat in a kitchen oven. They are also controversial.

Because of their relative newness, there has not been a long period of time in which these clays have been tested for permanence, for long half-life. Some doll makers feel that the new clays have not proven their stability and, because of this lack of guarantee of durability, refuse to work with them.

Others have more faith in modern chemistry and use the synthetic clays because of the greater flexibility they provide the sculptor. They are a perfect material for creating a sculpture which will be reproduced, as the sculpture can be baked hard and then will not distort in the mold-making process.

They are an excellent choice for the making of one-of-a-kind dolls, especially for satiric types whose exaggerated features would confound the most adroit mold maker.

Some find synthetic clays difficult to use at first. They often have a rubbery, springy texture which one must work against. Sometimes they are difficult to "get moving," until they have been warmed up to body temperature. Sitting on these clays is an excellent way to warm them up for use.

The most widely used synthetic clays are described below.

POLYFORM. This is the formal name for a white, rubbery clay also called SCULPEY. It is bakeable in a low-temperature oven. Sculptures can be added-to after cooking and rebaked. It can be sanded and painted with acrylic paints as it has an acrylic base.

SUPER SCULPEY. This is an improved version of Polyform. It apparently has a longer half-life and is easier for some people to work with. It ranges in color from cream color to light grey.

FIMO. This imported clay comes in small colored squares which are rather expensive. They can be mixed together to form almost any color desired. Mixing and blending take quite some time, as the clay is particularly difficult to "move" at first. Fimo dolls have a lovely almost-waxy, translucent color when they are properly done.

Because these clays have proven very popular, manufacturers will certainly be adding to this list. New doll artists might find it worthwhile to write to the manufacturer of any synthetic clay they may be contemplating using to find out its permanence before embracing it on a large scale.

# 27. Mary Hoot Polyform

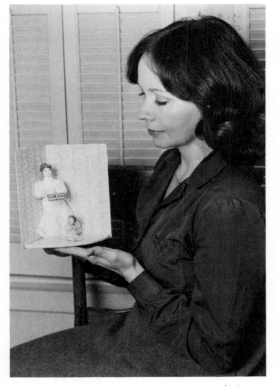

**Illustration 27-1.** Mary Hoot holding 1" = 1' (2.5cm = 30.5cm) scale hand-sculpted dolls.

Mary Hoot's doll making career began at the age of six when she sneaked a peach-colored sock from her mother's rag pile and fashioned a 4in (10.2cm) doll from it, complete with wardrobe.

She still has that first attempt. Her dolls have considerably improved since then, but she is still making miniatures.

She works in directly sculpted polyform and specializes in dolls of 1" = 1' (2.5cm = 30.5cm) scale. Each of her dolls is individually done; no molds are used.

The bodies are the same substance as the heads and are joined by stiff bendable materials. The hair is realistic but not real as the strands are extremely small, in keeping with the scale of the doll.

Most of Mary's dolls are inspired by someone real. They are lively little persons with animated expressions. Many of the persons depicted are very young. Sleeping and contented children are a specialty. Often Mrs. Hoot's granddaughter serves as a model for these. Portrait dolls and adults of all ages are also made.

Portrait dolls usually copy the exact clothing and accessories depicted in the photographs submitted by the client.

Among Mary Hoot's personality dolls are *Greer Garson, Emmett Kelly* and *Judy Garland.*

Mrs. Hoot strives to make her dolls as realistic as possible; she does not enjoy abstract work. The dolls are almost always doing something which adds to the illusion of reality. Because she uses real persons as models for her work, customers sometimes feel they have seen the person who is depicted. Sometimes that person is the customer himself, who sees in the doll himself at an earlier age.

Her costuming completes the dolls' illusion. It is designed and made by Mrs. Hoot to customers' preferences, with an emphasis on Victorian and Edwardian clothing which is elegant and formal.

Faces are meticulously painted in good detail. The Ohio artist will work indefinitely to get the features "just so." If she is satisfied, she knows others will be, also.

Mary Hoot has a strong motherly feeling toward her creations because of their realism and at times finds it hard to part with them. They are all her children, no matter how little they may be.

All Mary Hoot dolls and animals are signed and dated, usually on the surface upon which they sit.

Mary Hoot is a member of the National Association of Miniature Enthusiasts (NAME).

Illustration 27-2.  1″ = 1′ (2.5cm = 30.5cm) scale *Babies.* One-piece dolls of polyform. Mohair hair.

Illustration 27-3.  3½in (8.9cm) *Girl.* Polyform. Mohair wig. 4in (10.2cm) *Rag Doll* - - first doll made by Mary Hoot at age six.

Illustration 27-4.  6in (15.2cm) *Santa.* Polyform. Mohair beard.

# 28.  Oleta Hulen McCandless Fimo

**Illustration 28-1.** Oleta Hulen McCandless with her 1" = 1' (2.5cm = 30.5cm) scale dolls.

Oleta Hulen McCandless is a "fixer," a quality she traces back to her inventor father. She figures out new ways to put things together to come up with a superior product. This talent comes in handy when making miniatures. She is able to work out her own methods and speed up production.

Oleta's dolls, *Le Petit Ménage,* as she calls them, were once made of ceramic clay. Later dolls are made of Fimo, a synthetic clay, in a most unusual way. She has sculpted 12 to 15 different dolls and has made flexible molds for their heads, bodies, legs, arms and feet. Into these molds the Fimo clay is pressed. The molds are made to withstand the temperatures required to mature the Fimo.

The dolls are painted with an epoxy paint which the California artist mixes herself. The

body is all Fimo except for the upper arm and the thighs. These are padded wire. The hands are sculpted individually onto five-wire armatures, each finger being a wire. This enables the part of the doll which is usually the most fragile to be very strong and to assume any position dictated by the character depicted.

Hair is fashioned from an untwisted yarn used by weavers. It is 100 percent acrylic and comes in good hair colors. It takes a curl with a heated tool and will not straighten if exposed to dampness.

Mrs. McCandless uses synthetic fabrics usually to dress her dolls and compromises to meet the challenge of the intricate details used on costumes from the past. She stresses that the silhouette is the most important part. Details can be simplified or suggested by the proper

**Illustration 28-2.** 1" = 1' (2.5cm = 30.5cm) scale *Family Group.* Shoulder plates, lower arms and legs made of molded Fimo. Hands sculpted individually over wires. Cloth bodies on wire armatures. Synthetic hair.

Illustration 28-3. 5½in (14.0cm) *Madam and One of the Girls.* Breast plates, arms and legs made of molded Fimo. Hands sculpted individually over wires. Cloth bodies on wire armatures. Synthetic hair.

Illustration 28-4. 1" = 1' (2.5cm = 30.5cm) scale *Cook pretending she's angry with small boy.* Shoulder plates, arms and legs, torso of boy made of Fimo. Hands sculpted individually over wires. Cloth bodies on wire armatures. Synthetic hair.

use of trim. All of her dolls are dressed by her alone, and she never duplicates a costume except for that of the *Boudoir Lady,* who is dressed in a corset.

Her dolls run the gamut from wholesome families to madams and boudoir ladies. Costumes are from all eras, but Mrs. McCandless specializes in turn-of-the-century or Victorian dolls.

And what characters she makes: a fat cook, an old woman flower seller, workmen dressed

in overalls, children whose Dr. Denton sleepers are falling off, clowns, grandparents, servants and historical characters. All are realistic in their stances and can hold objects which characterize them, thanks to the strategic placement of wires in their construction.

In a sense, Mrs. McCandless' dolls are one-of-a-kind, since she never repeats, with the one exception, a character exactly, but she makes no such claim because many of them come out of the same mold. However, she does vary the painting of the faces and the hair. They are sold only fully dressed.

Mrs. McCandless says that she makes her dolls because of the continuing challenge they pose for her. She continues to experiment, always trying new methods, new ideas and new looks. She strives to produce a figure of heirloom quality that will, if given good care, look the same 100 years from now.

All McCandless dolls are signed and dated. The initials "O.H." and the date are found on the upper back, on the back of the calf or on the soles of the men's shoes.

Oleta Hulen McCandless is a member of the National Association of Miniature Enthusiasts (NAME).

Illustration 28-5. 1" = 1' (2.5cm = 30.5cm) scale *Pioneer Couple.* Shoulder plates, arms and legs made of Fimo. Hands sculpted individually over wires. Cloth bodies on wire armatures. Woman has flour sack "drawers" with "GLOBE A-I FLOUR" in faded colors on them. Synthetic hair. *Betty Martin Collection.*

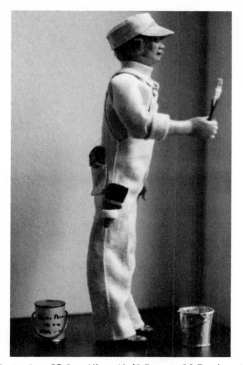

Illustration 28-6. 1″ = 1′ (2.5cm = 30.5cm) scale *Painter.* Shoulder plate, arms and legs made of Fimo. Hands sculpted individually over wires. Cloth body on wire armature. Synthetic hair. *Näda Richards Collection.*

Illustration 28-8. 1″ = 1′ (2.5cm - 30.5cm) scale *Clown.* Shoulder plate, arms and legs made of Fimo. Hands sculpted individually over wires. Cloth body on wire armature. Synthetic hair.

Illustration 28-7. 1″ - 1′ (2.5cm = 30.5cm) scale *Carpenter.* Shoulder plate, arms and legs made of Fimo. Hands sculpted individually over wires. Cloth body on wire armature. Synthetic hair.

Illustration 28-9. 1″ = 1′ (2.5cm = 30.5cm) scale *Dandy.* Shoulder plate, arms and legs made of Fimo. Hands sculpted individually over wires. Cloth body on wire armature. Synthetic hair. *Claire and Scotty Zion Collection.*

109

**Illustration 28-10.** 1″ = 1′ (2.5cm = 30.5cm) scale *The Maid: very prim, but not very bright.* Shoulder plate, arms and legs made of Fimo. Hands sculpted individually over wires. Cloth body on wire armature.

**Illustration 28-12.** 1″ = 1′ (2.5cm = 30.5cm) scale *Little Girl.* Shoulder plate, arms and legs made of Fimo. Hands sculpted over wires. Synthetic hair. *Näda Richards Collection.*

**Illustration 28-11.** 1″ = 1′ (2.5cm = 30.5cm) scale *Little Girl.* Shoulder plate, arms and legs made of Fimo. Hands sculpted over wires. Synthetic hair. *Toboloski Collection.*

**Illustration 28-13.** 1″ = 1′ (2.5cm = 30.5cm) scale *Gibson Girl School Marm.* Shoulder plate, arms and legs made of Fimo. Hands sculpted individually over wires. Cloth body over wire armature. Synthetic hair. *Sophie Dollarhide Collection.*

**Illustration 28-14.** 1″ = 1′ (2.5cm = 30.5cm) scale *Elegant Lady.* Shoulder plate, arms and legs made of Fimo. Hands sculpted individually over wires. Cloth body over wire armature. Synthetic hair. *Claire and Scotty Zion Collection.*

# 29.  Joann McCracken Polyform

**Illustration 29-1.** Joann McCracken and 6in (15.2cm) *Shop Keeper Doll.*

**Illustration 29-2.** 1″ = 1′ (2.5cm = 30.5cm) scale *Shop Keeper and Elderly Lady Shopper.* Shoulder plate, hands, feet of acrylic clay. Wire armature body padded with polyester fiberfill. Synthetic hair. Signed on feet.

**Illustration 29-3.** Detail of Illustration 29-2.

Joann McCracken makes no claims to be a fine arts doll maker. "I don't even know if my dolls belong in your book. I'm not sure how they fit in," she once stated. But her work has such charm and her methods of doll making are so ingenious, they merit study.

Her doll making began in 1972 as an offshoot of the successful business, Real Good Toys, that she shared at the time with John Javna. It specialized in wooden doll houses and toys. As there were no dolls to populate the houses, Joann drew upon her art training to design some which she could make on a relatively mass production basis to fill the void and accompany the houses to shows.

The designs were effective, and she soon had people working for her in her peak production periods who could follow her directions after she had made the initial sculptures, molds

**Illustration 29-4.** 1" = 1' (2.5cm = 30.5cm) scale dolls in *General Store. Photograph courtesy of Chilton Books.*

Clothing is built up in layers right over the padding, from the underpinnings out. Hardly a seam is sewn on any garment, as they are almost completely joined with fabric glue. This technique eliminates the need for hems and sidesteps the oversized stitches that are almost inevitable with hand sewing. Costuming this way is rapid and surprisingly pleasing. However, since it is done over the wires and padding of the doll's body, it becomes, in a way, the outer "skin" of the doll and it cannot come off. "The dolls' clothes are made of fabrics that are miniaturizations of real life size patterns," Joann states.

Her cast of characters is large and always growing as she does both multiples and one-of-a-kind dolls, the latter made on special

**Illustration 29-5.** 1" = 1' (2.5cm - 30.5cm) scale *New Englanders.* Shoulder plates, hands, feet of acrylic clay. Wire armature bodies padded with polyester fiberfill. Synthetic hair. Signed on feet. *Photograph courtesy of Chilton Books.*

**Illustration 29-6.** 1" = 1' (2.5cm = 30.5cm) scale *Toymaker and Boy.* Heads, hands, feet of acrylic clay. Wire armature bodies padded with polyester fiberfill. Synthetic hair. Signed on feet. *Photograph courtesy of Chilton Books.*

and patterns. Eventually, the doll making business overtook her, and she broke with Real Good Toys to concentrate on her own business, Joann McCracken's Dolls.

These dolls are flexible and nearly unbreakable and are constructed with easy, rapid methods which the Vermont resident has generously detailed in her book, *Dollhouse Dolls,* published by Chilton in 1980.

Her dolls' heads and limbs are made by pressing polyform into molds (Sculpey for heads and Super Sculpey for limbs). Thermostat wire is inserted into these pieces for armatures. Then they are baked until hard. The clay parts are painted with acrylic paints (since polyform is an acrylic clay), and the bodies are wrapped (padded with polyester fiberfill). The hair is made of natural fiber.

**Illustration 29-7.** 1" = 1' (2.5cm = 30.5cm) scale *Jazz Musicians.* Hands, heads, feet of acrylic clay. Wire armature bodies padded with polyester fiberfill. Synthetic hair. Signed on feet. *Photograph courtesy of Chilton Books.*

order. They range from Victorian children to shop keepers, jazz musicians and Santa Clauses. Ms. McCracken likes making character dolls the best but is also very interested in period costumes, so she constantly experiments to vary and improve her products.

These dolls are somewhere in between abstract and realistic. "The dolls do look like real people because almost every time someone sees them for the first time he says, "Oh, this one looks just like *so and so*," Joann reports.

She does not name any of her dolls unless she intends to keep them. "It is sort of like a child," she says. "The new parents should name the new member of the family."

Joann McCracken's dolls are sold in specialty shops, doll house shops and museum shops all over the United States. They are in the Atlanta Toy Museum.

Joann McCracken's dolls are marked with her initials (see below) and the date on the bottom of the foot.

**Illustration 29-8.** 1" = 1' (2.5cm = 30.5cm) scale *Peddler Doll.* Hands, head, feet of acrylic clay. Wire armature body padded with polyester fiberfill. Synthetic hair. Signed on feet. *Photograph courtesy of Chilton Books.*

**Illustration 29-10.** 1" = 1' (2.5cm = 30.5cm) scale *Victorian Lady.* Hands, head, feet of acrylic clay. Wire armature body padded with polyester fiberfill. Synthetic hair. 1981 prototype doll. Signed on feet.

**Illustration 29-9.** 1" = 1' (2.5cm = 30.5cm) scale *Baker.* Hands, head, feet of acrylic clay. Wire armature body padded with polyester fiberfill. Signed on feet. *Photograph courtesy of Chilton Books.*

**Illustration 29-11.** Detail of Illustration 29-10.

# 30. Susanna Oroyan
# Polyform

**Illustration 30-1.** 8in (20.3cm) *Elfreda* and 3in (7.6cm) *Elf.* Polyform bodies. Synthetic hair. Permanently affixed to base. © 1981.

Susanna Oroyan's dolls are piquant scrutinies of the dreams and foibles of mankind. The Oregon native makes dolls of all sizes, from miniatures to over-life-size, and works in, as she says, "any medium but kiln-fired clay."

Oroyan dolls are not play dolls, but what their designer terms "figures." They are fixed into position and are meant to interact with their environment in a predetermined way. Fragile creations, perhaps more sculpture than doll, they are not for everyone.

These are not pretty, vacuous dolly-faced creatures who will sit mildly on a shelf. Oroyan dolls are full of spirit and are ready to bring forth an ironic commentary. Indeed, they remind the viewer of the work of Daumier,

the great French caricaturist. Best known for his biting satires on contemporary 19th century French life which were done with crayon or brush, he also sculpted exaggerated satiric sketches which are now cast in bronze. These are near-doll-size.

Oroyan dolls are often commentaries on contemporary American society, on its foibles, its idols and its dreams. Subjects are not always pretty. There is a lot more commentary possible in a tart, a knave or a frumpy housewife in curlers and a housecoat than in a pretty lady, unless she is exaggerated so as to reveal the "real" person under the frills.

Literary and storybook character dolls are one of Mrs. Oroyan's strong suits. As with her social commentary dolls, these heroes are given often ascerbic interpretation and are brought to life with gentle irony, asking perhaps the question, "Where is the fine line drawn between the idol and the doll?"

Susie's work is seldom serious. She prefers to catch her subject unaware and to emphasize his tender points. Mouths are sometimes pursed, legs and arms elongated, positions

**Illustration 30-2.** Detail of Illustration 30-1.

114

**Illustration 30-3.** Detail of Illustration 30-1.

Polyform is the medium which enables Mrs. Oroyan to conjure up the lively expressions she wishes to capture. Its flexibility permits her to build long, slender fingers and noses and deep undercuts which would confound the most assiduous mold maker. Oroyan dolls are one-of-a-kind. Most have head and limbs of polyform clay with a wrapped wire armature body. Some of the tiniest are all polyform and are jointed at shoulder and hip.

While she enjoys sculpting and despises the tedious work of body making, her greatest pleasure in doll making is costuming. She admits to creating dolls as vehicles for her delightfully bizarre sense of dress design. These colorful outfits complete the personas which her sculptures begin. Unexpected shapes, colors and textures all work together to form a lively jigsaw puzzle whose pieces just seem to fall inevitably into place.

**Illustration 30-5.** 9in (22.9cm) *Miss Muffet*. Polyform head and limbs. Padded wire armature body. Synthetic hair. © 1981.

**Illustration 30-4.** 3in (7.6cm) *The Oldest Elf in the World*. Polyform. Synthetic hair. © 1981.

perhaps a bit undignified, all in the interest of capturing a cameo of human nature.

Although most of her dolls are permanently fixed into one position, some of her smaller dolls, especially her miniatures, are free spirits who can be positioned, within reason, by their owners.

Most Oroyan dolls are within the 15in (38.1cm) to 25in (63.5cm) size range. But what tiny dolls she does make are delightful.

**Illustration 30-6.** Detail of Illustration 30-5.

**Illustration 30-7.** 3in (7.6cm) *Dollies.* All polyform. Five-piece jointed bodies. Mohair hair. © 1981.

**Illustration 30-8.** 3in (7.6cm) *Dollies.* All polyform. Five-piece jointed bodies. Mohair hair. © 1981.

**Illustration 30-9.** 1½in (3.8cm) *Minna* by Susanna Oroyan. One-of-a-kind hand-sculpted doll of fired Fimo clay. Jointed with wires at shoulders and legs. Painted features, shoes, socks and underpants. Blonde dynel hair. Blue embroidery floss bow. Dress of white lace with blue sash. Marked: '81 Oroyan on back of left leg. 1981.

Mrs. Oroyan has won many awards, locally and nationally for her work. She has taught doll making on both the elementary and university level.

Susanna Oroyan dolls are signed and dated.

Susanna Oroyan is a member of the United Federation of Doll Clubs (UFDC) and the National Institute of American Doll Artists (NIADA).

**Illustration 30-10.** Susanna Oroyan at the ODACA banquet held in Santa Rosa, California, in March, 1981.

# 31. Faith Wick
# Polyform

Faith Wick is a one-woman doll making industry. She is enormously prolific and has sold, leased and licensed her designs to collectors and doll making concerns in the United States, Europe and the Orient. She works in sizes from 1in (2.5cm) to 30in (76.2cm).

Her doll making started with the life-size sculptures she made for a theme park which she and her husband once ran in Minnesota. The theme park is gone; the dolls remain.

Faith Wick makes, generally, character dolls which she describes in the following way: "I know the dolls that I like best have rather strange appearances and are different from most other dolls." It is this strangeness that sets them apart, making them readily recognizable.

Faith Wick specializes in characters and is best known for her witches, clowns and literary people. She has made hundreds of dolls, large and small, and in any given year she may design 50 or 500 one-of-a-kind creatures. They may be bag ladies, gnomes, children or portraits.

Her favorite character doll has been reproduced by Effanbee Dolls. Its name is *Wicket Witch.* The Minnesota artist tells why this is her favorite. "She reminds me of some of the people I knew as a child that were part of my growing up with foreign-born people. I loved them; yet their difference to me was a little fearful as a small child."

Mrs. Wick's early inspiration was Helen Bullard's book, *The American Doll Artist.* From the start, art dolls were the only type she wanted to create. Her first dolls were made of plaster, clay and cloth. She still works with these and has added porcelain and home-fire ceramics.

Many of her miniatures are made of polyform. Some are porcelain. They are not always 1" = 1' (2.5cm = 30.5cm) scale as the artist refuses to be restricted in the shape, size of subject matter of her output.

Sometimes the body is the same material as the head and limbs. Some have cloth bodies with armatures. Their hair may be sculpted to the head or made of mohair.

Her NIADA dolls are one-of-a-kind and are direct sculptures into a fired clay. Sometimes they are finished with wax and sometimes glazed.

Mrs. Wick is always experimenting and says she likes most about doll making "the freedom to express myself in a medium that allows the flexibility to use many materials" and she likes least "restrictions by contracts of certain types."

Some of her most important dolls were sculpted in unusual environments: in Greyhound buses, at doll shows or in restaurants.

Mrs. Wick has been fortunate to have many of her designs reproduced by commercial firms. At times, this procedure has watered down artists' work, and the resulting dolls have turned out nothing like the original concepts of their designers. At times, the dolls have been remarkably well done. When asked about her opinions on the way commercial firms have been reproducing artist dolls she replied, "I am satisfied with mine and from what I have seen and know about the industry, it is as well done as can be for a profit to be made." She believes that an artist can make a successful aesthetic and commerical compro-

**Illustration 31-1.** 1" = 1' (2.5cm = 30.5cm) scale *Santa, Mrs. Claus* and *Elves.* Polyform heads, lower limbs. Cloth bodies. Synthetic hair.

**Illustration 31-2.** 6in (15.2cm) *Henriette in rabbit suit.* Porcelain shoulder plate, lower limbs. Cloth body with wire armature.

**Illustration 31-4.** 6in (15.2cm) *Henriette as Clown.* Porcelain shoulder plate, lower limbs. Cloth body with wire armature.

**Illustration 31-3.** Detail of Illustration 31-2.

**Illustration 31-5.** Detail of Illustration 31-4.

mise in the production of her dolls by a commercial firm "if you are aware of the limits in the commercial field."

She considers her work to be not dolls but sculptures or "people figures." "The term 'doll' means something to be played with," she says, "and these are not . . . . From my point of view I have never made a doll but only small persons, wanting to recreate some part in history, (some) story in literature, a portrait of an interesting person and usually with humor."

Faith Wick considers doll making to be a fine art "depending on the skills of the doll maker and what the intent is in creating." Doll making to her is "an art form to be developed in its own right only if the collector recognizes an art doll for what it is and does not try to compare it with the lovely things that are truly dolls and are meant to be played with . . . The art doll is in its infancy, and I feel that I and my peers are pioneering in the field. We don't know except from what we do and others tell us if we are 'right' or not. It depends upon what success is measured by, money or pleasure."

Faith Wick's work has a wide public which is, perhaps, different from the norm. "My work tends to be appreciated and purchased by a certain group of people that are sophisticated art collectors and mostly by MEN."

In 1976, Faith Wick was selected as Minnesota artist of the year. She went to Washington, D.C., and met President Ford.

Faith Wick is a member of the United Federation of Doll Clubs (UFDC) and the National Institute of American Doll Artists (NIADA).

**Illustration 31-7.** Detail of Illustration 31-6.

**Illustration 31-6.** 6in (15.2cm) *Henry*. Porcelain shoulder plate, lower limbs. Cloth body with wire armature.

**Illustration 31-8.** 6in (15.2cm) *Emily No. 4.* Porcelain shoulder plate, lower limbs. Cloth body with wire armature.

119

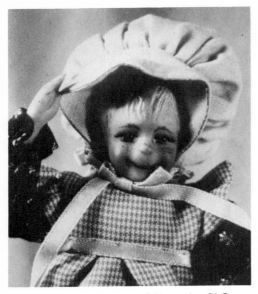

**Illustration 31-9.** Detail of Illustration 31-8.

**Illustration 31-11.** Detail of Illustration 31-10.

**Illustration 31-10.** 6in (15.2cm) *Eddie the Wizard*. Porcelain shoulder plate, lower limbs. Cloth body with wire armature.

**Illustration 31-12.** 6in (15.2cm) *Witch*. Porcelain shoulder plate, lower limbs. Cloth body with wire armature.

**Illustration 31-13.** Detail of Illustration 31-12.

**Illustration 31-14.** 1″ = 1′ (2.5cm = 30.5cm) scale *Witch.* Polyform hands, lower limbs. Wire armature cloth body. Synthetic hair.

**Illustration 31-15.** 6in (15.2cm) *Girl in Blue.* Porcelain shoulder plate, lower limbs. Cloth body with wire armature.

# 32. *Joann Williams*
## *Various Media*

Joann Williams works in a variety of synthetic clays, among them Fimo and bread dough. She creates charming, stylized one-of-a-kind figures, all of which are under 12in (30.5cm) in height.

She began making dolls in 1971 with the encouragement of Bess Fantl, founder of the Original Doll Artist Council of America (ODACA), who worked also in bread dough at the time. Mrs. Williams' formula for this medium is a mixture of white bread, white glue and acrylic paint. This is kneaded until it is like a fine clay, modeled and air dried. It is then painted with acrylic paints and sealed.

Bodies of dolls made in either Fimo or bread dough vary according to the subject depicted. Sometimes these are all-of-a-substance. Other times they have wire armatures with heads and limbs of the substance. Almost all dolls have movable arms and legs and can be posed. The hair is either modeled or made of thread.

Bread dough dries rapidly and becomes cracked under prolonged working, so dolls have to be deftly and quickly modeled. Sometimes, because of this, Mrs. Williams has found it necessary to rework her heads six or eight times to capture the effects she wants. She believes that hands are very important to the correct overall personas of her dolls and spends much time making certain they tell the story of the person she is depicting.

She has brought to life over 1,000 different lilliputians, many of them specially tailored to her customers' needs. She once created six figures for a miniature barbershop: a quartet singing "Sweet Adeline," a shoeshine boy and a man in a bathtub in the back room. Her dolls often tell a story, as in the case of the boy with a toothache who is trying to tell the dentist where it hurts. Sometimes they are literary characters, like *Dr. Fu Manchu,* or nursery rhyme people like *Little Miss Muffet.*

**Illustration 32-1.** 1¾in (4.5cm) *Campbell Kids.* All Fimo. Sculpted hair. Painted features. Felt clothes. © 1981.

**Illustration 32-2.** 1″ = 1′ (2.5cm = 30.5cm) scale *Clowns.* Heads and lower limbs of Fimo. Wire armatures. Cloth bodies. © 1981.

Williams dolls are a sort of mixture of abstraction and realism, technical proficiency and childlike naivete. They are busy little people re-enacting the world of today or yesterday or of unreality. They focus on a small corner of it that the viewer might have missed and bring it out for his inspection. And his smile.

Joann Williams dolls are marked:    J.W. 81 (or year made).

Joann Williams is a member and past-president of the Original Doll Artist Council of America (ODACA) and the National Association of Miniature Enthusiasts (NAME).

**Illustration 32-3.** 1″ = 1′ (2.5cm = 30.5cm) scale *Clowns.* Heads and lower limbs of Fimo. Wire armatures. Cloth bodies. © 1981.

**Illustration 32-4.** 1″ = 1′ (2.5cm = 30.5cm) scale *Soapbox Derby.* Head and lower limbs of Fimo. Wire armature. ©1981.

**Illustration 32-5.** 1¾in (4.5cm) *Easter Rabbit.* All Fimo doll with embroidery floss hair, painted features. Shown in decorated hen's egg. © 1981.

**Illustration 32-6.** 2in (5.1cm) *Miss Muffet.* All Fimo doll with embroidery floss hair. Painted features. © 1981.

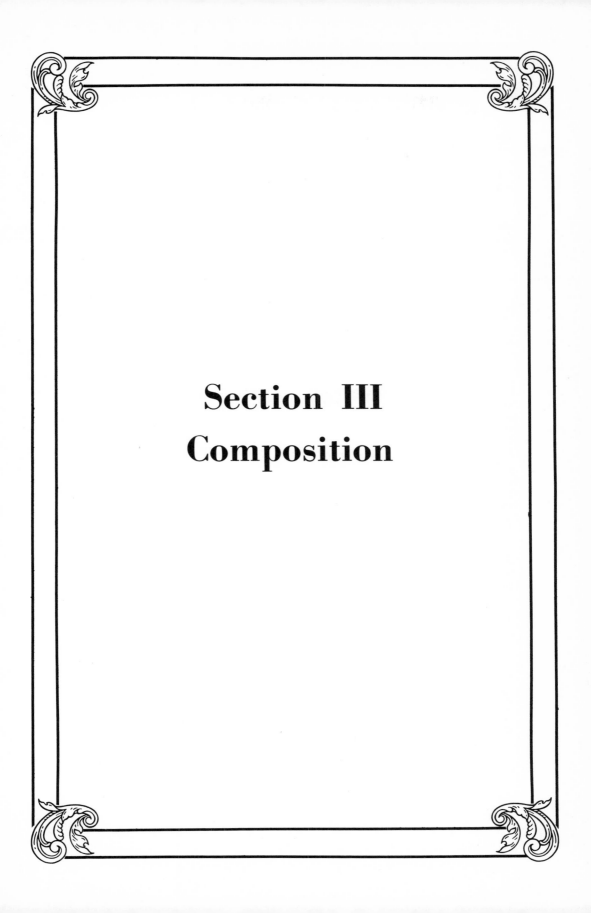

# Section III
# Composition

Composition is a catchall term without good definition. It is used for a variety of substances, all of which are "composed" by adding a list of materials together to form a compound from which a doll may be made.

Most solid compositions used by doll artists are secret combinations, the recipes for which they jealously guard.

The traditional composition which was used years ago, and which is still valid, was formed from fine, sifted sawdust, glue, clay and/or plaster, mixed together in varying amounts.

Today, some compositions use bread dough and glycerine as well as other ingredients. Bread dough composition, however, is susceptible to insect infestation and is not particularly permanent, even when sealed for protection.

Composition, commercially, was very popular between the first and second world wars, when the United States doll industry, which was not geared up for porcelain production, went into full swing. The composition then used was of the sawdust and plaster, or clay, and glue variety. This was generally pressed into molds, trimmed and painted. This material was cheap, lightweight, relatively durable, but the paint on these composition dolls flaked and cracked and disappeared in time.

Few doll artist dolls are now made of sawdust composition. Some use the traditional ingredients, but others use new discoveries.

A more commercial type of composition is a mixture of water, clay, liquid latex (a rubber-like material) and silicon. It can be mixed at home or bought in already prepared gallon or five gallon jugs. This "latex composition" is a "slip," which is water-based and pours, and it works in plaster molds, setting up very much like a porcelain slip. It is poured into the molds, allowed to set up and then decanted. Castings are removed, trimmed and filled and allowed to air dry until hard. Then they are sanded, painted with latex paints and finished.

Latex is hard on molds - - far more so than porcelain, but the latex composition doll has some factors which make it desirable. The chief one is resistance to breakage. Another is its relative lightness. A third is the relative safety for health that latex composition affords the doll artist, if one is careful not to breathe in the latex fumes when pouring slip into molds.

It is surprising, given these factors, that latex composition is not a more popular medium for the contemporary doll artist.

# 33. Sue Foucher Composition

Illustration 33-1. 1'' = 1' (2.5cm = 30.5cm) scale *Joanie, Greg, Karen, Mark* and *Trina*. Painted composition shoulder plates and lower limbs. Molded hair. Cloth bodies with wires inserted.

Sue Foucher comes from an artistic family. She has had many years of formal art training and works in numerous media. Watercolor and ink are her favorites. She started working in clay at the age of ten and went on to study dress design and painting.

At one time she designed stuffed dolls, but now she works in cast composition and makes doll house dolls in the 1'' = 1' (2.5cm = 30.5cm) scale. Adults are 6in (15.2cm) tall; children are 4in (10.2cm) to 5in (12.7cm) tall. Both portrait dolls and ''production'' dolls are in her line. For portraits she uses original sketches or front and side photographs to aid her.

Illustration 33-2. 1'' = 1' (2.5cm = 30.5cm) scale *Melissa, Rick,* and *Diane.* Painted composition shoulder plates and lower limbs. Molded hair. Cloth bodies with wires inserted.

**Illustration 33-3.** 1'' = 1' (2.5cm = 30.5cm) scale *Todd* and *Santa*. Painted composition shoulder plates and lower limbs. Molded hair. Cloth bodies with wires inserted.

The dolls' heads and limbs are sculpted in clay. From these sculptures, her husband makes molds for casting the composition slip.

After the parts are cast, they are sanded and readied for painting and glazing. Mrs. Foucher has developed her own paint colors which give to the composition the look of soft bisque. All dolls have sculpted and painted hair.

The dolls' bodies are made of stuffed cloth. Their limbs are wired to bend.

To date, the Michigan artist has created 18 different dolls. She tries to give each a distinct personality. Her costumes, all of which she personally designs, date from the 1800s up through the early 1900s. They are elaborate, in scale and beautiful.

Sue Foucher dolls are signed -S- on the lower back shoulder.

Sue Foucher is the past president of the Palette Guild, a well-known Michigan art club.

**Illustration 33-4.** 1'' = 1' (2.5cm = 30.5cm) scale *Young Man, Julie* and *Young Girl.* Painted composition shoulder plates and lower limbs. Molded hair. Cloth bodies with wires inserted.

**Illustration 33-5.** 1'' = 1' (2.5cm = 30.5cm) scale *Pioneers.* Painted composition shoulder plates and lower limbs. Molded hair. Cloth bodies with wires inserted.

# 34. Beverly Kidder
# Papier Mâché

Beverly Kidder of Princeton, New Jersey, is one of the few makers of miniature dolls who work in papier-mâché.

She builds her 1" = 1' (2.5cm = 30.5cm) scale dolls on wire armatures, one at a time. Sometimes the entire torso is molded from papier-mâché; sometimes it is done only to the waist. Then a cloth body is sewn and legs are wound with cotton and stretchy material. Hands and feet are of the same material as the head. They are modeled with details so that they look handcarved. Hair is either molded and painted or made of mohair.

All Kidder dolls are fully dressed in original costumes and depict characters from the middle ages to the 1920s. Historical and literary characters are a specialty, and they are made with an innocent charm.

Favorite dolls of this sort are *Sherlock Holmes* garbed in his dressing gown, *Dr. Watson* and the *Little Women.* The artist is always eager to work on special orders and welcomes the challenge of recreating a figure from the past.

**Illustration 34-1.** 1" = 1' (2.5cm = 30.5cm) scale *Doctor Watson* and *Sherlock Holmes.* Papier-mâché shoulder plates, lower limbs. Wire armature bodies. Modeled, painted hair. Holmes wears "silk" dressing gown. Watson has pipe in hand.

**Illustration 34-2.** 1" = 1' (2.5cm = 30.5cm) scale *Little Women.* Papier-mâché shoulder plates, lower limbs, wire armature bodies. Mohair hair.

Kidder dolls have an ingenuous air about them. They are in the tradition of good American folk art, and they remind the viewer of a cross between 19th century naive sculpture and 1920s Art Deco style. Somehow, the combination works.

Early Beveraly Kidder dolls are marked on the back with indelible red marking pen:

B. Kidder

(date - - prior to 1981)

After January 1, 1981, Kidder dolls are marked:

BJK

date

Beverly Kidder is a member of the National Association of Miniature Enthusiasts (NAME) and the Mini Tonga Society.

**Illustration 34-3.** Detail of Illustration 34-2.

**Illustration 34-4.** 1″ = 1′ (2.5cm = 30.5cm) scale *Victoria and Albert, their five oldest children and the Duchess of Kent.* Papier-mâché shoulder plates, lower limbs, wire armature bodies. Mohair hair.

130

# 35. Carol Nordell
# Composition

Carol Nordell's dolls are hard to pigeon-hole. She specializes in no one size or subject matter and works in several media. One pervading characteristic of her work is an excellence of design. The dolls seem to have a life, a presence. Even the smallest, which can dance on a penny, do so with a sureness and rightness of form.

Although they are pliable, they are fixed into set attitudes which reveal to the viewer something about the doll's intended psychology. In this way they, at times, resemble more a mixed media sculpture than a plaything. "Although they're flexible and jointed in the bodies," Mrs. Nordell states, "that's just for me until I can get them set in the poses that make them complete." This sculptural quality was recognized by the New Rochelle (New York) Art Association, when they awarded one of her dolls first place in sculpture at one of their exhibitions.

**Illustration 35-1.** 9in (22.9cm) *Marianne - - 14th Century nine-year-old girl with dog and garland.* Composition with wire armature. Scale: 2" = 1' (5.1cm = 30.5cm).©1980.

**Illustration 35-2.** 3/4" = 1' (2.0cm = 30.5cm) scale *Lady circa 1278.* Nylon stocking and wire armature. © 1980.

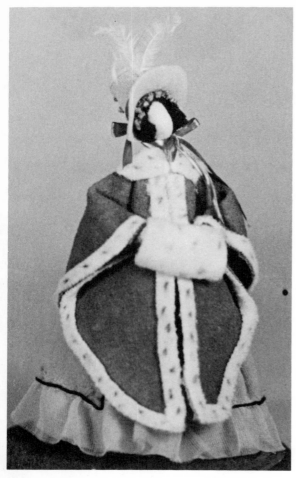

**Illustration 35-3.** 3/4" = 1' (2.0cm = 30.5cm) scale *1837 Lady.* Nylon stocking and wire armature.©1980

The NIADA artist's first doll making efforts were in two dimensions: elaborately, delicately frosted gingerbread cookie dolls. As time passed, she became interested in making miniatures and found that doll making books were right next to the miniature making books in the local library. In 1972, she made her first three-dimensional dolls. She tried many media, learning what she could from books and taught herself much by experimentation. She even learned to make molds but has never worked with ceramics.

Carol's first dolls were of a bread dough composition. Today (1981) she works primarily in her own special composition. She likes its warm, lifelike quality but is still striving to make it easier to work with. She is also interested in wax and experiments with it from time to time. Her tiniest dolls are a combination of many things, chiefly fabric, crepe paper and wire.

Many different kinds of work are involved in the completion of a Nordell doll. Some she prefers to others. "I'm not sure what I like best about doll making. Mostly it's the feeling when it's finished - - I love it - - such a complete, concentrated, palpable little entity."

Of all the steps in making her dolls, the modeling of the hands, faces and feet is the most demanding for Mrs. Nordell. She says, "I get so tired I can't wait to stop, until the creature gives me a certain look, and then I can't stop until I'm finished."

Mrs. Nordell's modeled work is in three scales: 1" = 1' (2.5cm = 30.5cm), 1½" = 1' (3.8cm = 30.5cm) and 2" = 1' (5.1cm = 30.5cm). She has made dolls in 3/4" = 1' (2.0cm = 30.5cm) scale, 1/2" = 1' (1.3cm = 30.5cm) scale and even smaller.

Most Nordell miniature dolls are in 1" = 1' (2.5cm = 30.5cm) scale. Many of her customers are miniaturists and want figures in this size to populate their houses. But she does not really regard herself as exclusively a miniaturist, and feels that the larger scale of some of her bigger dolls permits her to create some of her best costuming work.

The miniature dolls, as well as the larger dolls, run the gamut of characters. They have expressive faces and attitudes and almost always capture a sense of arrested motion. The remarkable thing about the work of this artist is that her very smallest dolls, which range from 1½in (3.8cm) to 3in (7.6cm) in

**Illustration 35-4.** 1" = 1' (2.5cm = 30.5cm) scale *Jo - - Edwardian six-year-old with jump rope.* Composition with wire armature. Mohair hair.©1980.

Illustration 35-5. 3/4" = 1' (2.0cm = 30.5cm) scale *Odile*. Nylon stocking with wire armature. Rear view. ©1980.

Illustration 35-6. 3/4" = 1' (2.0cm = 30.5cm) scale *Odile*. Nylon stocking with wire armature. Front view.©1980.

size, also display these qualities, even though they are too small to have faces.

The miniature dolls start with a jointed skeleton of taped copper wire as heavy as will work for the size doll she is making. Fingers are modeled around fine copper wire. The skeleton is built out by padding and wrapping with strips of quilt batting and nylon stocking fabric. Small gathered scraps of the panty part of panty hose are stuffed and sewn in places where she needs bulges.

The tiniest dolls use finer wire, of course, and are wrapped with narrow strips of nylon, crepe paper or used fabric softener sheets. Her finest copper wire comes from a rotten light cord.

Illustration 35-7. 9in (22.9cm) *Wili*. Composition with wire armature.©1981.

Nordell fashioned a group of medieval Christmas ladies. For the 1981 convention, held in St. Louis, Missouri, she executed a series of 26 dancers that illustrate the theme, "Dancing From A to Z." Another group brings to life operatic characters. She wants to someday do a series of elves and fairies.

Mrs. Nordell believes that doll making is a fine art - - or a mixture of fine arts. It is the constant need for artistic choices of color and line that makes her certain of this. "Not all doll making is a fine art . . . but if they're made with fine art they become fine art dolls," she asserts.

Most Carol Nordell dolls are signed on tiny strips of very thin white leather which are glued to a petticoat hem or somewhere else inconspicuous. Many Nordell dolls are permanently affixed to their bases, so they need no identification other than the sign on

**Illustration 35-8.** 3/4" = 1' (2.0cm = 30.5cm) scale *Maria Taglioni.* Composition on wire armature.©1981

The miniature dolls are harder to make than larger ones in some ways, she reports, and easier than others. It is easier to "cheat" - - to get an effect with some little thing; a few details go a long way. It is harder, though, to make the materials behave.

This she does superbly. Her miniature dolls' garments drape and fall as if they were full size. Yet some of these dolls are barely more than 1in (2.5cm) in height. "I'm not interested in making a doll and letting someone else costume it. I want to do the whole thing," she explains.

Carol Nordell dolls are definitely one-of-a-kind. They have no set subject matter. "I'm constantly aware of the diversity of humanity. I guess I could say that what I'm trying to do is to celebrate the truth that we are all created differently yet all have much in common," she reports. "Maybe I could get rich if I stuck to one thing or type but I don't want to do that - - it's getting late."

Carol does mostly commissioned dolls - - some as portraits, some inspired by paintings. But she prefers to work out her own ideas. Often she will create a group of dolls that enact a certain theme. For the 1979 convention of the United Federation of Doll Clubs (UFDC), held in New York City, she made a group of New Amsterdam folk. The 1980 UFDC Convention, held in Washington, D.C., had as its theme "Christmas in July." Mrs.

**Illustration 35-9.** 1/4" = 1' (0.65cm = 30.5cm) scale *Maria Taglioni.* Wrapped wire. Standing on a penny. © 1980.

the base. Most of the dancers are too bare or too small to hide a label on them.

Carol Nordell is a member of the United Federation of Doll Clubs (UFDC) and the National Institute of American Doll Artists (NIADA).

**Illustration 35-11.** 1/4″ = 1′ (0.65cm = 30.5cm) scale *Fanny Ellsler*. Wrapped wire. Standing on a penny.Ⓒized1980.

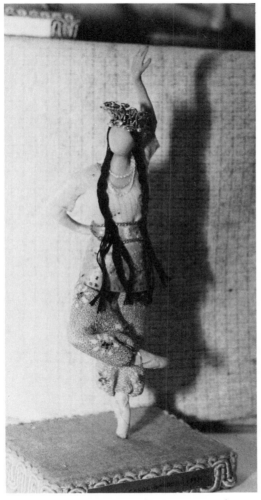

**Illustration 35-10.** 3/4″ = 1′ (2.0cm = 30.5cm) scale *Queen*. Composition on wire armature.Ⓒ1981.

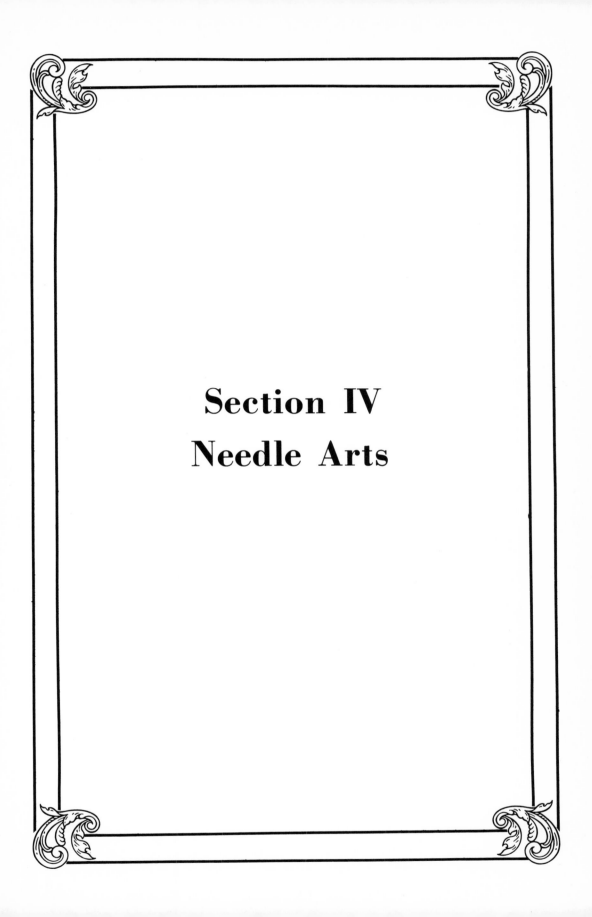

# Section IV
# Needle Arts

How difficult it is to generalize about a subject as broad as the needle arts! Artist dolls have been made using virtually every needle technique known.

Every doll artist needs to be proficient with a needle. He needs to know how to draft patterns, shape bodies and make clothes. Some need these skills more than others.

The needle artist, obviously, needs the most skill of all, for his product relies solely upon his prowess with needle and thread. He may work with knitting, crocheting, cross stitch, needlepoint, virtually every known facet of tailoring and sewing to make his final product.

Probably some techniques have been invented just for dolls. "Needlesculpture" seems a good candidate. Needlesculpture is usually done on a supple, knitted material. Nylon stockings are popular. The artist props a bit of stuffing behind the stocking and sticks his needle in and out and shapes features with it right on/in the stocking. He prods and pokes and pinches and pleads and finally comes out with a face that is unlike any other. Needlesculpture is usually quite large. It takes great skill to make a miniature doll with it.

Probably the first dolls of many a doll artist were rag dolls. Fiber and needle are familiar tools, especially for the woman artist. But for the product to rise above the level of the ordinary rag doll, for it to take on a quality of grace, style and aesthetic composition takes talent and practice. To do this successfully on a miniature scale using materials meant for much larger scale products is very difficult.

# 36. Audrey Jean Caswell
## Crochet

Audrey Jean Caswell fabricates some of the smallest original needle-worked dolls in captivity. They are crocheted and range in size from 3/4in (2.0cm) to 3/16in (0.46cm).

These diminutive persons are meant to be dolls for a doll house family 1'' = 1' (2.5cm = 30.5cm) to play with. They are so tiny that they are in perfect scale for model railroad H.O. Gauge Fezzwigg metal doll furniture. Yet each doll has movable, poseable arms and legs and is intricately dressed.

Mrs. Caswell is a self-taught doll maker. Although she only knew a few basic crochet stitches and still cannot read a crochet pattern, she began experimenting with different crochet hooks and threads to design some clothes for her 1½in (3.8cm) antique all-bisque dolls. When she had finished those outfits, she still had many ideas for other clothes and no more dolls to dress, so she began to make dolls to fit the clothes.

She chose wood for the heads because she has always liked "penny wooden" dolls and clothespin dolls. After several experiments she ended up with a doll that was a miniature replica of what a mother might make for her little girl. She put it under a doll house Christmas tree. Then she made another doll that she put into one of her little girl's doll house dolls' arms. Soon her ideas and talents took over, and she began making dolls from all nations.

Some of Mrs. Caswell's dolls are: 3/4in (2.0cm) *Mr. and Mrs. Santa Claus* and elves; 3/4in (2.0cm) *Heidi* and *Peter,* 3/4in (2.0cm) Tyrolean children; *Juan* and *Marie,* 3/4in (2.0cm) Mexican children; a family 1/2in (1.3cm) to 3/16in (0.46cm) including grandmother, grandfather, father, mother, teenage girl, little girl, doll, little baby boy, maid and butler. She makes a nativity scene 1/2in (1.3cm) to 3/16in (0.46cm) which includes Mary, baby Jesus, Joseph, white king, Latin king, negro king, shepherd and angel. Other dolls are 3/4in (2.0cm) *Helen,* a fashionably dressed lady with a large hat with roses on it;

3/4in (2.0cm) *Cathy,* a little girl type doll; 3/4in (2.0cm) *Baby Jean,* a baby with a long white dress trimmed with roses and a frilly bonnet; and 3/4in (2.0cm) *Dean,* a man wearing a suit and tie and sporting a moustache.

The dolls' heads are wood. Their hair is mohair and the rest of the doll is crocheted. Their clothes are their bodies, although Mrs. Caswell intends to also make a 3/4in (2.0cm) doll with removable clothes and wardrobe.

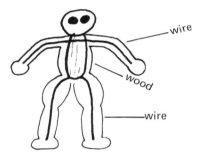

**Illustration 36-1.** Audrey Jean Caswell holding miniature doll house populated with her tiny dolls, and doll house family, which won ribbons at the 1980 UFDC convention held in Washington, D.C. Around her neck she is wearing the locket with miniature dolls in Illustration 36-3 in it.

**Illustration 36-2.** 3/4in (2.0cm) *Baby Jean.* Crocheted doll with long white dress trimmed with roses, frilly bonnet. Head is a painted bead. Mohair hair. Shown in a locket.

**Illustration 36-3.** 3/4in (2.0cm) each: *Cowboy* and *Cowgirl. Cowboy* wears big cowboy hat, has a gun in a holster and a lariat in his hand. *Cowgirl* dressed in "Sunday" clothes. Both have crocheted bodies, clothes, mohair hair, painted beads for heads. Shown in a locket.

**Illustration 36-4.** 3/4in (2.0cm) *Helen.* Fashionably dressed lady wears hat with roses on it. Dressed in shades of blue. Crocheted body, clothes. Painted bead head. Mohair hair. Shown in a locket.

Caswell dolls are a combination of wood and crochet. Because they are so tiny, painted wooden beads are used for heads. Light pink-orange beads are used for caucasian dolls, light brown for black dolls and tan for Hispanic dolls. White beads are for china dolls and dark orange resemble antique painted bisques. Facial features are dots like on the old "penny wooden" dolls. They are made with a 5-0 pen point; this is the only size that looks right on such a tiny head.

The body of the doll is a piece of wooden toothpick covered with crocheting. Arms and legs are crocheted with a brass wire inside them so they can be moved. The hands are painted to match the heads.

A No. 14 crochet hook and different types of sewing thread are used in the crocheting. The different thicknesses of thread determine the finished size of the dolls. All this work must be done under a magnifying optical loop. Even then the artist can hardly see the 3/16in (0.46cm) dolls.

Their hair is mohair. Some dolls have long curls; some have long straight hair. The men and babies have short curly hair.

The doll's body is its clothing - - and what clothing it is. These tiny persons are dressed to the minutest detail. The cowboy wears blue "denim" pants, holster, and cowboy hat. His cowgirl friend has a yellow rose of Texas embroidered on her skirt. Lady dolls have long crocheted pantalets, hats and intricate embroidery. The Texas artist intends to make larger dolls, also. A 2in (5.1cm) baby doll which will have removable clothes and a complete layette,

and a 5½in (14.0cm) peddlar doll with wooden carved hands, feet and head are among the first of her plans. The peddlar's "wares" will be tiny dolls and other crocheted items, of course.

Caswell dolls are too small to sign. The artist encloses a card with each doll listing the doll's name, number, date made and her signature.

## Dolls
### by Audrey Jean Caswell

Helen #14
October 1980
Audrey Jean Caswell

**Illustration 36-5.** 1/2" = 3/16" (1.3cm = 0.29cm) *Nativity Scene: Mary, Baby Jesus, Joseph, Caucasian King, Latin King, Black King, Shepherd and Angel.* Crocheted bodies, clothes, mohair hair. Painted beads for heads.

**Illustration 36-6.** 1/2" = 3/16" (1.3cm = 0.29cm) *Family: Maid, Girl with doll, Girl, Mother with Baby, Father, Son, Grandma and Grandpa.* Crocheted bodies, clothes, mohair hair, painted beads for heads.

Mrs. Caswell is a member of the United Federation of Doll Clubs (UFDC) and the National Association of Miniature Enthusiasts (NAME).

**Illustration 36-7.** 3/4in (2.0cm) *Mrs. Claus, Santa* and *Christmas Tree.* Crocheted tree. Crocheted bodies on dolls, clothes. Painted beads for heads. Mohair hair.

**Illustration 36-9.** 3/4in (2.0cm) *Helen* and *Dean.* Crocheted bodies, clothes. Painted beads for heads. Mohair hair.

**Illustration 36-8.** 3/4in (2.0cm) *Heidi, Juan* and *Marie.* Crocheted bodies on dolls, clothes. Painted beads for heads. Mohair hair.

# 37. Margaret Finch
# Cloth, Wood

**Illustration 37-1.** 9in (22.9cm) *Betsy Ross.* Direct hand-carved wood head, neck, forearms and hands. Wrapped wire armature.©1976.

Margaret Finch is one-of-a-kind and so are her dolls. This NIADA artist's motto is "never more than one," thus insuring that each of her creations is as much an adventure for her as it is for her customers.

She describes herself as one of the "loners not cloners" among doll makers. That is, every aspect of her work is done by her alone. She does not merely design her creations and pass on the ideas to others to execute as some

"mass production" doll artists do. This would defeat the whole purpose of doll making for her.

Doll making to Mrs. Finch is an art form, a means of expressing her feelings in a personal, tactile sense - - a form of sculpture. This is why she calls her work "Fine Art Dolls." She strives with them to help raise the level of understanding of the general populace that a doll can be a work of art - - that fine doll makers are really creating sculptures, not playthings. This is why she is justly proud that one of her dolls won second place, *sculpture category,* at the juried annual show of the New Rochelle (New York) Art Association.

Sculpture is a family tradition for the New York State resident. Her uncle was the sculptor, Frederick W. MacMonnies. When she was in her teens, she visited his studio and drank in its lessons. Her brother is a sculptor. Her daughter, Marta Finch Kozlosky, has continued the family pattern. She has chosen one of her mother's media - - wood - - and become a doll artist in her own right, creating beautiful finely-carved fully-jointed all-wood dolls.

Mrs. Finch works in two media, needle-modeled cloth and directly-carved wood. Her dolls are explorations of ideas and themes and at times are the incarnations of dreams. She is interested in conveying a sense of lightness and of arrested motion in her figures through the interaction of poses and fabrics. Above all, she hopes to impart to her viewer a sense of visual pleasure.

Some Finch dolls can be termed "historical." They embody the essence of a time period without slavishly depicting any one particular personage or fashion. Mrs. Finch may spend weeks steeping herself in the time period she wishes to recreate. When she is done, she so thoroughly has learned its visual music that she can freely interpolate its themes. The dolls she thus creates express a time and place (usually pre-20th century) as filtered through her insight.

This inclination for invention is carried further by her fantasy figures, the *Phantasmata,* gentle beings which spring forth from her imagination. They are creatures of wonder with only slight ties to the world of rational man. Crossbreeds from another dimension of time and reality, they are concoctions of strange beauty and elegance posessing such human and animal characteristics as suit their mystic needs.

Finch dolls seem to fall into series. The above-mentioned *Phantasmata* made of needle-modeled cloth or wood are up to 8in (20.3cm) in height.

*Winky Walnut:* This is the only doll done in an edition, a tiny wire-and cloth baby in a walnut shell. Each time it is done it becomes more elaborate. Perhaps 15 to date have been completed.

MUMSHINS: These miniature size dolls are no taller than 8in (20.3cm). They are seldom character or portrait dolls; more often they are period dolls. Most mumshins are little girls of the 18th or 19th centuries. They have

**Illustration 37-2.** 8in (20.3cm) *Phyllis Wheatley, poetess-slave, 1776.* Direct hand-carved wood. Wrapped wire armature.

names such as *Jennifer Lane, Sally Good* and *Dora Dear,* as each one is a real person to its creator.

FINE ART DOLLS: These dolls are made in two sizes: under 8in (20.3cm) and from 12in (30.5cm) to 15in (38.1cm). They are made of cloth or wood. The smaller dolls are often very glamorous ladies of past centuries. For example, *Daphne Fair,* in silk georgette, about 7in (17.8cm) tall, is dressed for a ball given in New England in the 1840s. She wears pale blue silk, has a wreath of green leaves entwined in her hair and carries a little bouquet of violets complete with gold ribbon streamers. Her pendant necklace is a genuine ocean pearl. Her tiny satin slippers have hand-painted designs, and her white stockings have embroidered cutwork. Her delicate fingers, all separate (wrapped wire), have applied fingernails.

Larger Fine Art Dolls are also wood or needlemodeled cloth with painted faces. These are the dolls upon which Mrs. Finch can best indulge her fancy, for the size permits more intricate detail.

*Images of the Goddess:* Mrs. Finch describes this series as "dolls expressing the

**Illustration 37-3.** 8in (20.3cm) *Dragonfly Lady.* Silk chiffon skin. Needlemodeled, wire armature. "Jewel" eyes. Carries a dagger because dragonflies are "the cruelest of insects." An insect on/in her rosy lips.

**Illustration 37-4.** 9in (22.9cm) *Phantasmata No. 3: "I have heard the mermaids singing, each to each."* Needlemodeled cloth on wire armature. Blue net skin. Hair of various colors of green, gold, blue pastel organdy and deep green "seaweed." Varied shades of green-gold in the beads in hair and wrapped around her body. Tail of iridescent hues of green, rose and blue. Tail fin of dark green and rose. Green metallic fingernails. Comb and mirror of "antiqued" gold and pearl. © 1981.

various archetypes from what I feel to be the basic feminine process or stimulus, the 'eternal feminine' which remains constant through her various mutations, all through the history of religion, which is, after all, the history of the human race."

Currently, the NIADA artist is most interested in pursuing her *Phantasmata* and *Images of the Goddess* series. She prefers not to work on commission, but to work out her own concepts and present them to the public. In this manner, she can let her imagination and serendipity take over. She claims that her dolls "just seem to happen."

When she begins carving a wooden doll's head and torso she makes no models or sketches, but just "digs in" and the resulting doll head usually turns out to be just about right. Using this method, she does not adhere to one size or work to a strict scale as some doll makers do. "The dolls sort of create themselves. They are the size they want to be," she says.

After the hands, feet and any exposed skin of the doll have been carved of wood, they are painted. The artist then drills holes into the wood and glues in a copper wire armature. After thorough drying, the armature is wrapped with fabric, perhaps a stretch knit.

The doll is then dressed, always from the legs and feet up and out. All underpinnings, according to the period depicted that might be visible after the doll is completed, are executed before the outer garments are made. As she does not work from plans, she must repeatedly and laboriously keep draping the figure with the full set of materials that will appear on the finished doll in order to see if she is heading in the right direction. When the costuming is done, a wig is prepared.

Finally a stand is built and covered with materials to suit the doll. Mrs. Finch spends a surprisingly long stretch of time positioning the doll in exactly the way she wants it. She pays particular care to the "motion" of the fabrics and succeeds in capturing a feeling of vitality and energy quite often because of this.

Her needlemodeled cloth dolls are done in a similar extemporaneous fashion. "I don't even use sketches for any of my dolls," she says. "I make them up as I go along, unless, of course, I'm working from a painting or photograph."

Cloth dolls are built up on different types of wire - - usually pipe cleaners, because they do not have to be wrapped for slippage. The

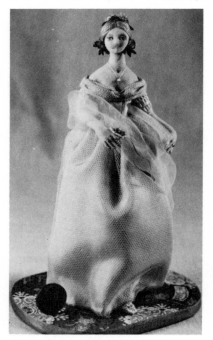

**Illustration 37-5.** 7in (17.8cm) *Daphne Fair.* Needlemodeled cloth. Wire armature. Wears pale blue silk taffeta ball gown circa 1840. Vine leaves in light brown hair. A genuine ocean pearl pendant. Carries a bunch of violets. Has hand-painted white satin "ballerina" slippers, petticoats trimmed with eyelet embroidery. Separated fingers.

top skin of silk georgette is added to several underlayers of cloth. Then the face is painted and later needlemodeled. The costuming procedure is the same for all Finch dolls.

Mrs. Finch's pleasure in her doll making is apparent from the following description: "Margaret of Anjou . . . was the first doll where I had a real feeling of 'taking off,' of real excitement born of sensing, from the first twisting of the wires, the full flavor of the completed figure - - it's hard to explain."

This delightful attitude towards the nature of her materials and dolls has resulted in a cast of spirited characters that at times do seem to have wills of their own.

Margaret Finch believes strongly that doll making in America is capable of developing into a fine art if it has not already reached this stage. She cites the Japanese as an example to emulate. They have long recognized the artistic status of the doll maker and have named a leading maker of art dolls as a "living national treasure." She feels that the more often doll artist work can be displayed as sculpture and compete as sculpture in art shows the better. "If we persist," she says, "we're bound to win

**Illustration 37-6.** 7in (17.8cm) *Daphne Fair.* Close-up of Illustration 37-5.

**Illustration 37-7.** *Dora Dear, circa 1840.* Needle-modeled silk chiffon, painted features. White stockings. Red garters. White lawn pantalets and upper petticoat with crocheted edge. Tan flannel petticoat. Tan leather slippers, blue bows. Blue and white striped lawn dress, buttoned down back, lace collar and cuffs. A wide orange silk chiffon scarf for sash. Tiny brooch, red bead. Carries a sprig of blossoms.

out. I think our position in the doll world will only be enhanced by acceptance by the art world."

Inasmuch as they are not the sole creations of the artist who conceived them (her criterion for an artist doll), she feels that commercially produced dolls can never be art dolls. "How can a work of art, created with enthusiasm,

love, endless patience, etc. ever be reproduced commercially? I can't bear to have someone else help me . . . so how could I bear to have some manufacturer - - even myself - - compromise, and compromise would be inevitable, of course; it's the nature of the beast."

The doll world is fortunate that Margaret Finch disdains compromise.

Each Finch "Fine Art Doll" is individually named and carries a description card, and is numbered. Each Finch doll comes with a NIADA certificate.

Margaret Finch is a member of the United Federation of Doll Clubs (UFDC) and the National Institute of American Doll Artists (NIADA).

**Illustration 37-8.** 7in (17.8cm) *Charlotte Ames, circa 1650, Jamestown, Virginia*. No. 3 in *Our Ancestors* series. Needlemodeled silk chiffon, painted features, separated fingers. A pert, gay, fashionable young woman in the colonial capital. Dark green stockings, lilac clocks, gold-tipped orange satin ribbon garters, blue-green leather shoes, red heels, silver binding, lilac rosettes. Knee-length chemise, beige linen under-petticoat, pale green silk petticoat with burnt-orange fringe; dark red silk over-petticoat with gold ribbon trim; pale rose silk satin gown, back-laced and seams overlaid with gold galloon; lace-trimmed chemise sleeves; stomacher laced with green ribbons; wide Vandyke lace collar tied with black bows. Black hair, coiled back twisted with red ribbons and bows of the same. Lace-edged head scarf fastened with gold-headed pins. Attached to her waist by pea-green and dark blue-green cords are her engraved octagonal silver mirror and her light-green feather fan, silver mounted. Drop pearl earrings, pearl choker and diamond brooch with triple pearl drops. Three gem rings.

# 38. Beverly Port
# Fabric, Porcelain, Wax, Composition

Beverly Port combines media to create creatures from childhood dreams and fantasies. She describes her dolls as "realistic, fantasy and character dolls."

Her forte is the depiction of memory beings, dolls which evoke dreamy, happy memories of years gone by. They may be soft-bodied, acrylic-painted dolls with human hair that display a gentle nostalgic air or characters from favorite stories, such as *Ozma* and the *Lavendar Bear King* from Frank L. Baum's *The Lost Princess of Oz,* or *Puss-in-Boots* or *Time Machine Teddies,* which recall the earliest 20th century plush bears.

The Port Orchard, Washington, artist works in porcelain, wax, cloth and composition, choosing the medium or media necessary to convey the concept she wishes to materialize. She uses unexpected juxtapositions of media, colors and textures that somehow work perfectly to highlight each other, forming a complementary whole.

*Tedwina* and *Tedward,* two of her plush bears, have porcelain snouts. *Puss-in-Boots,* a regal cat-doll, combines porcelain, fur, wool and pheasant features for an elegant overall effect. His *trompe l'oeil* porcelain fur on the realistic cat-head fools many a viewer. *Bearby,* a doll inspired by a photo of Beverly's little niece in a teddy bear Halloween costume, has a porcelain child's face, glass eyes, a plush body (with thumbs on its hands) and is fully jointed.

Her dolls are often engineered in quite complicated, painstaking ways so that they will "work." She has devised a difficult swivel-neck apparatus for a wax cowboy doll of hers - - swivel necks are seldom seen on wax dolls because of the problems encountered when one wax surface rubs on another. Mrs. Port's *Pinafore Pals* doll is a half-and-half doll of high-fire porcelain bisque in which one side is a black girl and the other white. The process for making this doll is particularly exacting because the two colors of the porcelain must be joined at just the right time. In 1977, the artist obtained a United States patent for this process, so she is officially an inventor. Some

**Illustration 38-1.** 5in (12.7cm) *Theodore B. Bear.* An eminently qualified teddy bear author made of old wool cloth in a warm brown color with button eyes and blue flowered vest. He is fully jointed. Shown writing his articles at his wooden desk with his telephone handy. © 1974. Limited edition.

dolls have rotating hip and arm joints, some have wire armatures for complete posing. And teddy bears are completely jointed with swivel necks.

Beverly makes two types of dolls: "primary figures," in which no mold is used, and "artist editions," which are very limited

147

**Illustration 38-2.** 3-1/8in (2.8cm) *Love Bears.* Golden brown porcelain bisque with black eyes, noses and mouths. Jointed with wires at arms and legs. Modeled like "old fashioned" teddies with long arms and humps on their backs. Wear red hearts on ties around their necks. © 1977.

**Illustration 38-3.** 5in (12.7cm) *Mandy.* (Also made 3½in [8.5cm] to 4in [10.2cm] tall.) Brown cloth with hand-painted face and curly fur wig. Her face is needle-molded around a special face section. Complete outfit of dress, petticoat, pantalets and pinafore. © 1974.

**Illustration 38-4.** 6in (15.2cm) *Father Christmas.* Porcelain head and hands. Painted, glazed eyes. Wire armature in body. Bends at knee and elbow. Velvet outfit trimmed with real fur, handmade holly. Leather boots. Holds miniature candy canes, stocking of velvet and long staff. Comes in custom-made box with antique-looking Christmas tree on cover. © 1980.

editions. Her dolls range in size from 1½in (3.8cm) to 48in (121.9cm). Her miniature dolls vary in height and she does not rigidly adhere to the 1" = 1' (2.5cm = 30.5cm) scale, although she has made many dolls in that size since she began in 1970.

They cover a wide spectrum of media and subjects from an old fashioned 6in (15.2cm) tall *Father Christmas* with porcelain face and hands and wire armature body to a 5in (12.7cm) tall cloth black child named *Mandy* who has a hand-painted face that is needle-molded around a special face section. She wears a curly fur wig.

Mrs. Port likes to work in several styles and use a variety of materials to keep her interest fresh.

She is somewhat a pioneer in the championing of the animal doll and of the teddy bear as an art form. Her interpretations of Teddy are fresh and unusual and continually surprising. Her first original bear, the 5in (12.7cm) tall *Theodore B. Bear,* was designed as an accessory to her large porcelain doll, *Percy,* who dangled him by the arm during the

**Illustration 38-5.** 3in (7.6cm) *Dolly, the Two-Face.* Cloth doll. Fur wig. Face with open eyes has glass eyes. Sleeping side has painted eyes. Wire armature in body for complete posing and bending. © 1974.

**Illustration 38-6.** 8in (20.3cm) *Turn-Head Teddy.* Old curly white mohair. Fully jointed. He has a tail that can be pushed back and forth which makes his head turn side to side. Limited edition. © 1980.

**Illustration 38-7.** 7½in (19.1cm) *Candy Container Teddy.* Old red wool mohair with felt paws and foot pads. Fully jointed. Head turns, lifts off to reveal candy container inside body. Hump on back. Limited edition. © 1980.

**Illustration 38-8.** 6½in (16.5cm) *Tiny Teddy.* White wool and mohair happy little old-fashioned bear. Fully jointed. Swivel neck. Long curved arms. Hump on back. Limited edition. ©1980.

**Illustration 38-9.** 8in (20.3cm) *Bearby.* Porcelain face with painted, glazed eyes. Fully jointed doll-bear with thumbs on its hands. Also made in 4in (10.2cm) size. Limited edition. © 1976.

1974 convention of the International Doll Makers Association (IDMA) in Reno, Nevada, at which he won first price for porcelain. *Theodore B. Bear* has gone on to become a star reporter and spokesbear for his fellow teddy bears through his writings in *Bernice's Bambini* and the 1976 UFDC winter issue (the teddy bear issue) of *Doll News,* the association's official publication.

His success encouraged Beverly to design bears in other substances and styles. She makes them of plush, porcelain, velvet, mohair and artful combinations of these and other materials. Always, they are intricately jointed to move and behave as bears should. Some of her bears are muffs or candy containers; some are on wheels. Big and small, hard and soft, sombre and bright, they provide the artist with an unending source of inspiration.

Mrs. Port explains her choice of subject matter very simply. "I create things that I *enjoy* and other people enjoy them, too."

Beverly Port dolls are marked with a label in the shape of a large letter B with the doll's name, the copyright date and BEVERLY PORT on it. A few labels are oval.

Beverly Port is a member of the United Federation of Doll Clubs (UFDC), the Original Doll Artist Council of America (ODACA), the National Association of Miniature Enthusiasts (NAME) and the Good Bears of the World.

**Illustration 38-10.** 7½in (19.1cm) *Patches, the Teddy Bear with a Secret.* Also made as large as 23in (58.4cm) tall. Porcelain, sculpted face. Glass or painted, glazed eyes. Body of colorful patchwork velvet. Fully jointed. He has a secret compartment and "growler" in his body. © 1976.

**Illustration 38-11.** 4in (10.2cm) *Tedwina* and *Tedward.* Also made as large as 18in (45.7cm) tall. Twin baby bears from the *Four Bears Family.* Original, sculpted porcelain faces. Painted, glazed eyes. Plush bodies. Fully jointed. Holding *Jester Bear* rattles by Kimberlee Port. Limited editions. ©1976.

# 39. Kimberlee Port
# Fabric

Kimberlee Port began making her miniature bears in 1976, when she was 16 years old. Her aesthetic combinations of colors and materials remind one of her mother, Beverly Port's, doll making talents, (which see), but her imagination and sense of humor are distinctively hers.

Kim's bears range in size from 1/2in (1.3cm) to 8in (20.3cm) and are made of a short plush fabric. They are completely jointed with swivel heads. All Miss Port's designs are completely original. She makes her own patterns, the bears themselves and their costumes.

Her range of characters is wide. Among them number *Santa Bear, Bear Elf, Bearina the*

*Fashion* (who has a swivel neck, wire armature body, and displays a lace parasol and a trunk for her wardrobe), *Bearterflies* of unexpected colors, *Bairy, Hobear, Yankee Doodle Bear* and *Bitsy Bear*. Eight-inch (20.3cm) *Mama Bear,* in her stylish maternity bonnet with lace trim has a tummy zipper topped by a white

**Illustration 39-1.** 8in (20.3cm) *Santa,* 7in (17.8cm) *Mama: The Teddy Bears' Christmas.* Created especially for *Doll News,* Winter, 1976, cover. Short, fine gold-color plush bears. *Mama* and two young bears standing have wire armatures in bodies making them completely poseable. Others are jointed. All have swivel necks and black button-like eyes. Completely hand-sewn and finished even to tiny buttons and buttonholes. Made when the artist was 16 years old. © 1976.

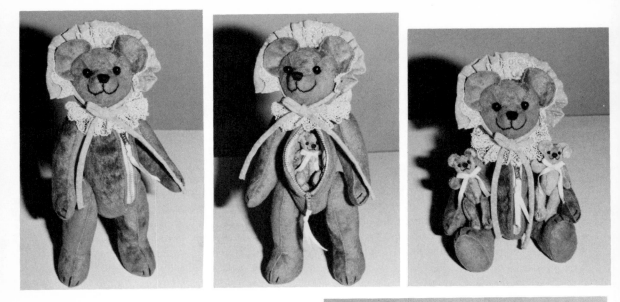

**Illustration 39-2.** 8in (20.3cm) *Mama Bear.* Short, fine plush. Wears maternity bonnet with lace trim. A white satin ribbon trims her tummy zipper. Unzip zipper and out peeps (Illustration B) a baby boy bear of blue. Illustration C: He is followed by a pink girl. Both are felt. Babies are 2½in (6.4cm) long. All fully jointed with swivel necks. © 1977.

**Illustration 39-4.** 2½in (6.4cm) *Baby Bear.* Short, fine gold plush. Fully jointed with swivel neck. Wears blue lace dress and pantalets. Blue bow by left ear. Heart-shaped tag. © 1976. *Peter Bull Collection.*

**Illustration 39-3.** 7in (17.8cm) (approximately) *Hobear.* Short, fine plush. Has swivel head, wire armature body. Completely bendable including at elbows and knees. Has pockets on his "top hat and tails." His knapsack contains tiny dishes and has comb for combing his fur. All clothing removable. © 1977.

ribbon. When it is opened, a baby blue boy bear and a pink girl bear emerge - - each 2½in (6.4cm) tall. All are fully jointed and have swivel necks.

Miss Port's work has appeared in various doll magazines. Among them are *Doll News, Doll Revue, Bernice's Bambini, Living Dolls* (England) and UFDC national and regional souvenir books. She designed the cover of the 1976 UFDC winter issue of *Doll News* - - the teddy bear issue.

Her bears and dolls are in several museums.

Kim Port's bears are identified by a heart-shaped label with the name of the teddy, KIM PORT and the copyright date on it.

Kimberlee Port is a member of the United Federation of Doll Clubs (UFDC).

**Illustration 39-6.** 8in (20.3cm) *Baby in a Basket.* Large baby bear of short, fine, gold-colored plush. Fully jointed with swivel neck. Wears christening outfit. Has ruffle-edged quilt to keep her cozy in her basket-bed. Also has been made in smaller and larger sizes. © 1979.

**Illustration 39-5.** 7in (17.8cm) *Bearina, the Fashion.* Short, fine gold-colored plush. Wire armature inside body to make her completely poseable. Swivel neck. Dress and bonnet lace trimmed. Tiny parasol. Trunk lined in same fabric. © 1976.

**Illustration 39-8.** 1¼in (3.2cm) *Bitsy Bears.* In a variety of teddy bear colors. Felt. Fully jointed, including swivel necks. Hold tiny candy canes. Tiny bows on necks. Come in custom-made boxes with Kim's heart trademark tag on cover. © 1976. *Christmas Elf Bears* in background (see Illustration 39-9).

**Illustration 39-7.** 2½in (8.9cm) *Bearterfly,* 1¼in (3.2cm) *Bairy* and 2in (5.1cm) *Bairy Horse. Bearterfly,* a brightly-colored fanciful felt bear with brightly-colored wings. Antennae on head. Flower and ribbon around head. Fully jointed with swivel neck. *Bairy and Bairy Horse* (both with wings) also in felt. © 1979.

**Illustration 39-9.** 2½in (8.9cm) *Christmas Elf Bears.*
Completely hand-sewn bears with red or green suits.
Shoes with pointed toes and tassels, hats of contrast-
ing color. Various bear colors. Fully jointed. Swivel
necks. Arms and legs have wire armatures so they can
bend at knees and elbows. Hats are removable. Have
tassels at tips. Tiny braid trim on hat, at neck, wrists
and ankles. © 1978.

**Illustration 39-10.** 4in (10.2cm) *Mama Rabbit.* Fully
jointed grey fabric rabbit with swivel neck. Embroidered features. Dressed in calico. © 1978.

# 40. *Joanne Marion Scott (Jarion)*
# *Needlesculpture*

Needlesculpture, if not deftly handled, can produce coarse, grotesque dolls. In the right hands, biting, satiric or gently humorous ones can be created. Joanne Marion Scott's work is the latter.

Her doll world is populated with tiny beings from a world of dreams and fantasy. They range from 1in (2.5cm) to 5in (12.7cm) in height and are needlesculpted from nylon hose over cotton-stuffed wire armature bodies. Their hair is fashioned from unraveled lopi wool.

Each of her little people has a distinct personality. Among the types represented are gnomelings, elves, witches, fairies, Scottish dancers, figure skaters, brides and grooms, mothers and babies, guitar players, elfin pipers and medieval ladies.

No two dolls are the same, and the artist makes varying interpretations of each theme.

They are dressed with imagination and flair. Each little creature's garments are entirely hand-sewn from the delicate underpinnings to the leather shoes. The choice of color and fabric is bright and unexpected and effective.

**Illustration 40-2.** 5in (12.7cm) *Witch and Gnome Lady.* Needlesculpted nylon stocking with wire armatures.

**Illustration 40-1.** 5in (12.7cm) *Medieval Lady.* Needlesculpted nylon stocking. Wire armature body. Silvery metallic flower-printed dress and hat with overlay of dark blue. 1980.

155

**Illustration 40-3.** 4in (10.2cm) *Musician* and *Gnome Lady*. Needlesculpted nylon stocking with wire armatures.

**Illustration 40-4.** 5in (12.7cm) *Ice Skaters and Gnome Lady*. Needlesculpted nylon stocking. Wire armature body.

Jarion dolls are only sold fully dressed, as the costuming is integral to their personalities.

They are most appealing and look as if they are waiting to join in the next fairy ball. To think that such pedestrian materials as Joanne Scott uses can weave such extraordinary folk!

Each Jarion doll has a circled capital Ⓙ embroidered on the back of it for identification.

# 41. Susan Sirkis Fabric

**Illustration 41-1.** 7½in (19.1cm) *1830 Bride.* Stockinette-covered, padded wire armature. Painted with polymer resin coating for protection. Features painted in acrylic. Hair of mohair. One-of-a-kind.

Susan Sirkis dolls are like an animated fashion book. Since 1973, she has recreated in cloth the styles and attitudes of the past, distant and not-so-distant. Specializing in no particular era, her creations include historic figures like *Queen Elizabeth I, Empress Elisabeth of Austria, Angelica Van Buren, Marie Antoinette* and *Joan of Arc.*

Figures from paintings by famous artists like Gainsborough (*Pinkie* and the *Blue Boy*)

and Goya are made in three dimensions. Fashion plates are also brought to life, as in her 1830s bride.

At times, Sirkis dolls are whimsical but yet sophisticated. Such characters as *Tubby,* a well-coiffed lady in the bath sipping champagne(?), a mermaid, and a well-undressed *Lady of the House* who is depicted seated on a brass bed in the process of removing a stocking in a well-practiced alluring way.

Fashion is perhaps a keynote of Mrs. Sirkis' work. She describes her dolls as "beautiful people - - perhaps unrealistic in their visual perfection." She makes many lovely ladies and children who are exquisitely dressed. Much care and exhaustive research is necessary to achieve the degree of authenticity exhibited by these dolls. Everything is correct, in scale and in proportion - - and very elegant.

At first glance it is difficult to ascertain Mrs. Sirkis' medium and method, as her techniques and results are unusual. Her dolls, however, are made of fabric, and the technique is a form of needlesculpture - - done in a very special way. The dolls are made over a wire armature, wrapped and padded with cotton and yarn, and covered with a cotton stockinette "skin." They are then painted with a polymer resin coating to protect the fabric. The features are done in acrylic, and the hair is curly mohair.

Sirkis dolls are one-of-a-kind as she does not work from a mold, and each figure is individually crafted. She has, at times, made duplicates. The dolls are available only as completed figures. Mrs. Sirkis has made some naked ladies, including *Lady Godiva* and the *White Rock Girl,* but these cannot be dressed.

The Virginia woman is well-known as a designer of and an expert on doll clothing. Each of her *Wish Booklets,* of which there are 23, deals with some aspect of doll making or dressing. She lectures and writes extensively for books and magazines.

Susan Sirkis dolls are signed in various places but are all marked "Susan Sirkis," and the year.

Susan Sirkis is a member of the United Federation of Doll Clubs (UFDC) and the National Association of Miniature Enthusiasts (NAME).

**Illustration 41-2.** 7½in (19.1cm) *Egyptian Lady.* Stockinette-covered, padded wire armature. Painted with polymer resin coating for protection. Features painted in acrylic. Hair of mohair. One-of-a-kind.

**Illustration 41-3.** 7½in (19.1cm) *Elizabeth I.* Stockinette-covered, padded wire armature. Painted with polymer resin coating for protection. Features painted in acrylic. Hair of mohair. One-of-a-kind.

# 42. Carol Sligh
## Fabric

Carol Sligh combines colors and textures and paints to produce whimsical fabric dolls. She is unsure of how many hundreds of characters she has brought to life, but her supply of ideas seems bottomless and outruns the amount of time she has for their execution.

They range in size from the little 1½in (3.8cm) ones that balance on doll stands made from a fabric snap and a pin to 18in (45.7cm) tall. Since 1975, the greater part of her work has been in doll house scale.

The Holland, Michigan, doll maker has been working with fabric since she took sewing in 4-H. Her dolls began life as one-of-a-kind stuffed Christmas ornaments. She showed them to a store owner in New York City who specialized in miniatures who asked if she did doll house families in cloth. She went home and changed her production to dolls.

Sligh dolls are made of unbleached muslin. The artist makes up a pattern, draws it onto the material, sews it, turns it right side out and stuffs it. Then she paints the faces which are flat and reminiscent of old-fashioned cloth dolls and next applies hair. This is made of whatever she finds and thinks will work and look the way she wants it to. Yarn, embroidery floss, fringe, and silk buttonhole twist are all used. She dresses them to her fancy. At first the dolls were contemporary. But the Victorian costuming proved so popular that the doll maker has leaned increasingly toward it.

Her range of characters is wide. She makes Victorian women, children, babies, 1½in (3.8cm) dollies and circus performers. She makes newborn babies in sacques, older babies in bonnets and dresses, ballerinas, tennis players, *Orphan Annie,* black dolls and children in pajamas. Her tiniest dolls have the same diversity: mermaids, harem girls, Indians, *Little Bo Peep* and sheep, and *Red Riding Hood,* to name a few.

The freshness of their hand-painted faces and the juxtaposition of the textures of fabrics used for clothing and hair fibers give a lively surface to these soft sculptures. Their characters are done with a gentle, reminiscing, humorous touch.

**Illustration 42-1.** 6in (15.2cm) *Victorian Circus Performer.* Unbleached muslin. Hand-painted features. Doll still unfinished when photo taken. Pin in left hand. © 1981.

The artist prefers to make one or two of a kind only. As each doll is individually done, no two are actually identical. "If I'm making little Victorian boys or girls I'd rather make a little group, all different, for a customer to choose from. Ideally, though, I should make more than one to utilize the time and ideas that went into each doll," the artist says.

Besides the 1″ = 1′ (2.5cm = 30.5cm) scale dolls, she also makes a series of little girls which are more simply made and a little taller (maybe 6in [15.2cm] to 6½in [16.5cm]).

159

"I think life is vastly interesting and can't see how anyone could ever run out of things to do or interest them," says Mrs. Sligh. The diversity of her production attests to this.

Carol Sligh dolls are signed with a small cloth label, usually somewhere under a garment. Most say "Carol Sligh," but a few of the tiny tiny ones have just "Sligh" attached.

Carol Sligh is a member of the Original Doll Artist Council of America (ODACA).

**Illustration 42-3.** 5½in (14.0cm) rear view of Illustration 42-2.

**Illustration 42-2.** 5½in (14.0cm) *Female Victorian Biker.* Unbleached muslin. Hand-painted features. © 1981.

**Illustration 42-4.** 6½in (16.5cm) *Male Victorian Biker.* Unbleached muslin. Hand-painted features. © 1981.

Illustration 42-5. Rear view of Illustration 42-4.

Illustration 42-7. 5in (12.7cm) *Portrait Doll.* Sister of Illustration 42-6. Unbleached muslin. Hand-painted features. Embroidery floss hair. © 1981.

Illustration 42-6. 5in (12.7cm) *Portrait Doll.* Unbleached muslin. Hand-painted features. Embroidery floss hair.

Illustration 42-8. 1" = 1' (2.5cm = 30.5cm) scale *Potty Chair Babies.* Unbleached muslin. Hand-painted features. Boy has embroidery floss hair. Girl has mohair hair. © 1981.

**Illustration 42-9.** 5in (12.7cm) to 5½in (14.0cm) *Kate Greenaway-type Dolls.* Unbleached muslin. Hand-painted features. Mohair wigs. © 1981.

**Illustration 42-10.** Rear view of Illustration 42-9.

162

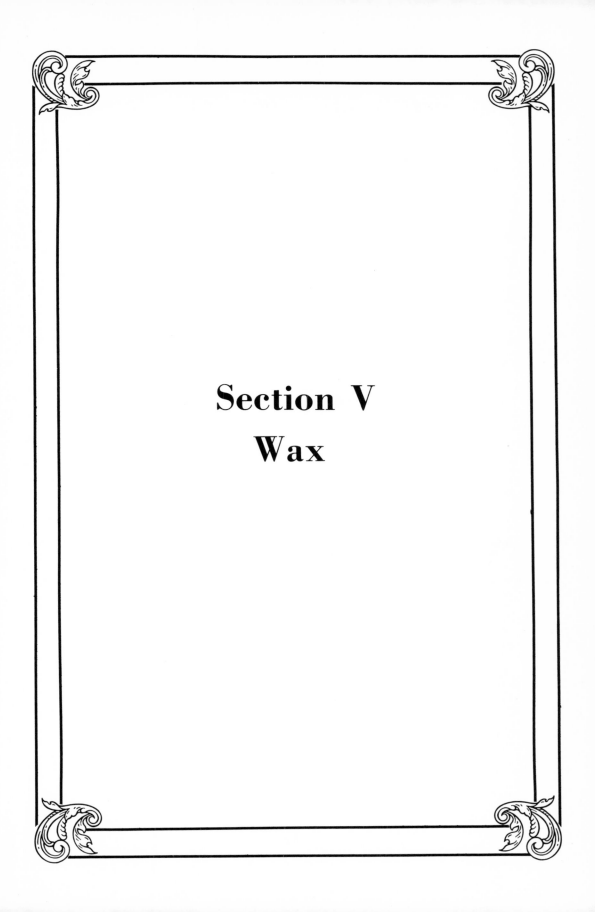

# Section V
# Wax

Wax has been a doll making medium, not to mention a sculpting medium, for centuries. Its ability to change states - - from solid to liquid and back - - and the sculpting options it affords: modeling, carving and casting are why it is a favorite of sculptors.

Most often, however, for permanence, statues that are sculpted or modeled in wax are cast into other materials, notably metal, by the "lost wax" (*cire perdu*) process. Here, the wax sculpture melts and is drained away, after a casting mold is made of it for the pouring of hot metals.

In the 19th century, wax came into the spotlight as a doll making medium when, in mid-century, the English doll makers, Montanari, produced their wax dolls, which captured the public's imagination at the Crystal Palace.

Wax has a wonderful, lifelike translucence that no other medium can match. It has a lifelike feel, too, and is comfortable when kept in temperatures which humans enjoy.

However, the public has certain fears which are really unjustified about wax dolls, against which doll artists must struggle. Chief of these is a concern about permanency. "Will it melt?" are words which make a doll artist grit his teeth. One might ask a porcelain artist, "Will it break?" or a fiber artist, "Will is soil?" Of course, it will, but not if care is taken. Modern doll artists have perfected techniques for rendering their wax as permanent as possible. They concoct special mixtures of different waxes and chemicals and binders. Then they use any of several procedures to give the wax an inner core of strength.

They may employ what is called the "wax-over" method. This was popular in the 19th century, when composition was used as a base for wax dolls. The heads were immersed (several times, if needed) in the liquid wax until it built up to the thickness desired. Sometimes the composition dolls were painted with rather garishly bright colors which, after the application of the wax, became impressively natural looking. Composition is still used as a base for wax-over dolls although the skin tones are usually added to the wax into which the composition is dipped. Clay and porcelain are other popular bases for contemporary wax-over dolls.

A popular method for making wax dolls is the casting of liquid wax into molds made directly from the artist's sculptures. These are usually of plaster or latex with a plaster outside shell to hold the mold pieces together. Hot wax is usually poured in and decanted in a similar process to porcelain with strict regard to temperature and safety. Then, for permanence, often liquid plaster is poured into the molded doll's head, making sure that the shoulder plate area is still hollow enough to accept a cloth body underneath.

Dolls can be carved out of a block of specially formulated wax which has been rendered durable with additives. They can also be directly modeled for one-of-a-kind works.

With all of the options available to the doll artist, it seems strange that more do not work in wax. In part, it is because until recently, with the publication of the excellent book, *Modern Wax Doll Art*, on wax technique by ODACA artist, Carol Carlton, little information on wax doll making was available. In part, it is because materials, in particular such substances as microcrystalline wax, are not readily obtainable, especially to doll makers in outlying areas (which seems to be almost everyone). In part, it is because of the mystique of wax work. It has an almost spooky connotation to some (shades of Madame Tussaud's). It seems like it is more difficult to work in than it is.

Most of all, there is that public resistance to work against. Porcelain artists have the same problem, to a lesser extent. What is needed for the wide acceptance of wax dolls is a greater awareness of just what a wax doll is. This is accomplished by a long, slow educational process.

People who buy wax dolls know why they buy them and what they are. They are works of art.

# 43. Doreen Sinnett
## Wax, Polyform, Porcelain, Fabric

Doreen Sinnett's approach to doll making is businesslike. She works in several media and creates miniature dolls that are only partially finished, so that her customers can have the satisfaction of completing them. Almost everything is in 1'' = 1' (2.5cm = 30.5cm) scale.

Each doll making idea is intended to fill a void Mrs. Sinnett detected in the miniature world and each is, at least partially, a project which requires the active participation of the purchaser for its completion.

Her first effort was a set of silk-screened doll house people. Printed flat, they were designed to be colored, sewn together and stuffed like pillows, then embellished with stitchery.

She later designed a set of clothes patterns and directions for making 1'' = 1' (2.5cm =

**Illustration 43-1.** 1'' = 1' (2.5cm = 30.5cm) scale porcelain doll house dolls. All are Doreen Sinnett originals with the exception of the reproduction Pouty doll, marked with *. China painted porcelain shoulder plates, lower limbs. Wire armatures. Cloth bodies. Mohair hair.

**Illustration 43-2.** 1'' = 1' (2.5cm = 30.5cm) scale doll house dolls with the first of Doreen Sinnett's two-part molds for making dolls from Super Sculpey. Three versions of *Doll No. 792M.* Heads and limbs of Super Sculpey. Wire armatures. Cloth bodies. Mohair hair. Seated doll in *Ruth Pettigrew Collection.*

30.5cm) scale clothespin dolls. These had modeled features and movable bodies. Rather than sell finished dolls, she marketed instructions for making them.

A line of doll house doll clothing patterns followed. Then came sculpted dolls. These were at first made in wax-coated composition. About a dozen heads were designed and were cast as kits (heads and limbs of wax-over-composition). The dolls were available two ways: either as kits, with body and clothing patterns provided, or undressed with fully-poseable wire armatured cloth bodies.

She has extended her media to include porcelain and casts her designs in high-fire

**Illustration 43-3.** 1″ = 1′ (2.5cm = 30.5cm) scale doll house *Man*. Wax-over-composition head, torso, limbs. Balance of body is cloth with wire armature.

**Illustration 43-4.** 1″ = 1′ (2.5cm = 30.5cm) scale *Woman*. Wax-over-composition head, torso, limbs. Balance of body is cloth with wire armature.

slipcast porcelain bisque. These are available in the same format as the wax-over-composition.

Her realistic characters include several men and ladies, a black or Hispanic couple, an elderly couple and children. The dolls' hair is made of mohair and wigs are individually styled. All dolls are made to order with coloring and hair styles the choice of the client.

In 1981, the California doll designer offered molds of her doll house dolls which were intended to be used with Super-Sculpey, a low-fire synthetic clay, so that the home doll maker could reproduce Sinnett designs at home. This carries the Sinnett doll making philosophy to its logical conclusion.

One divergence from the dolls designed for customer completion is a delightful 5in (12.7cm) tall gnome made of wax and only made completely bodied and dressed.

Doreen Sinnett is a member of the United Federation of Doll Clubs (UFDC) and the National Association of Miniature Enthusiasts (NAME).

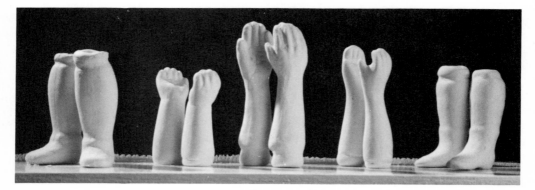

**Illustration 43-5.** 1″ = 1′ (2.5cm = 30.5cm) scale unpainted doll house doll limbs. Wax-over-composition.

# 44. Sheila Wallace Wax

Sheila Wallace creates modern wax dolls that are works of art and labors of love. Historic portraiture is her specialty, and she breathes life into the long-dead names and faces that stare from the pages of history books. To Sheila Wallace history is neither dead nor dull; it is people and personalities filled with fascination.

She seeks, with her work, to bring these individuals once more to life, to give them concrete form. "The characters (in history books) were real people - - they're real to me. History has become personalized," she explained in an interview. This enthusiasm is evident in her work, for her creations have vitality and personality.

Long years of European training as a portrait artist form the basis of her skills. After completion of the General Certificate of Education exams in art at both the ordinary and advanced levels in Devon, England, she studied painting, drawing, sculpture and fine arts at the Heatherly School of Fine Art, completing her art education with a concentration on sculpture and anatomy at the City and Guilds Art School in London. She also studied with the craftsmen of Madame Tussaud's waxworks. This intensive training forms a broad basis from which she can draw in her doll making.

Although Ms. Wallace has been interested in costume dolls for quite some time - - she had the idea to do a costume doll of Marie Antoinette when she was only 13 years old - - doll making was not foremost in her mind during schooling. The Pennsylvania artist trained to be a sculptor. "I did not go to school to learn to make dolls," she explains. "I do not think there are any such schools. I sort of invented techniques on my own."

It was while she was working as a secretary in London, doing commissions in her spare time, that doll making worked its way into the sculptor's life. She began making plaster of paris dolls, but soon her father convinced her to work in wax. After much research into traditional methods of wax sculpture, she hit upon a formula which is based on one used by European wax modelers of the 17th century.

**Illustration 44-1.** 1" = 1' (2.5cm = 30.5cm) scale *Gibson Girl*. Cast wax shoulder plate, limbs. Wire armature body. Doll designed to be sold expressly by Kimport Dolls. ©1980.

The old methods, however, have been adapted and improved.

The modern dolls have heads, hands and sometimes lower limbs modeled from bleached beeswax. They are solid wax, unlike the old dolls which were either hollow, having been cast from molds, or dipped wax, over papier-mâché. Because of this the heads are impervious to freezing, whereas the old ones were not. And the sculpted dolls are surprisingly durable. Since the melting point of beeswax is 125°, they can be kept easily in the average home.

The balance of the doll is other materials. Ms. Wallace constructs a wire armature for the figure to allow it flexibility in posing. Over this she builds a cloth body filled with polyester fiber. Most often lower limbs are constructed

**Illustration 44-2.** 6in (15.2cm) *Baby Angel.* Head, arms and legs of cast wax. Cloth body filled with polyester fiber with copper wire skeleton inside. Mohair hair.

of composition, with footgear fitted to the foot, not molded-on.

When the body is complete, the hair on the head, eyebrows and the hands (of male dolls) is individually implanted, by needle, into the wax. The faces are then painted with either oils or watercolors, in accordance with the styles of cosmetology prevalent at the time the individual lived. Ms. Wallace is particular about accuracy in this matter and researches each time period and its styles thoroughly before commencing a project. In fact, before each doll is begun, she spends a great deal of time ascertaining the correct physiognomy, costuming and life-style of the person to be depicted. Whenever possible, she prefers to work from death masks or contemporary portraits of the individual. Most dolls are historical figures "not just because I am superstitious of making dolls of living people, but because I prefer to work on subjects with more general appeal, and I love historical costume."

Costuming is meticulous and time-consuming, but a favorite aspect of the process for the artist. It presents many challenges, the most demanding being those involving scale and materials. "Scale is so important to costuming," the artist noted. "You can learn about costumes from seeing the originals in museums, and you get a feel of the period." But modern fabrics are difficult to use in designing period costumes. "Today everything is made for

durability and is washable. People do not wear damasks or brocades anymore."

Cloth made from all natural fibers is more and more difficult to find, and fabrics that will fall properly and give the correct impression of the full-scaled antique ones are nearly impossible to come by. Modern synthetics make washing easy and pressing effortless, but these qualities are an enormous obstacle to the doll artist who is striving to create an 18th century person with accurate and permanent folds in his costume.

Concepts about clothing have drastically changed since the time of Marie Antoinette, one of Ms. Wallace's favorite subjects. Many of the garments of that time could neither be washed nor cleaned and clothes definitely "made the man," describing his station in life for all to see. The Pennsylvania artist prefers to only depict those people whose clothing has something to say. She notes that for the nobility, costumes were worn as symbols of class or position, not necessarily for warmth and convenience. And some of these clothes were certainly elegant.

"Most of my clothing is hand-sewn in order to be authentic," stated the doll maker. "I do, sometimes, use the sewing machine, but only where appropriate - - in other words, on costumes dating from a time when the sewing machine was in general use. I do all the work myself, from the doll, through the costuming, even to the stands. I'm very independent."

Although her larger dolls are her best-known work, her miniature dolls, which range in size from a 6in (15.2cm) baby to 1" = 1' (2.5cm = 30.5cm) scale doll house dolls, are made in the same way. Unlike her larger portrait dolls which are directly sculpted in wax, however, these small ones are done in multiples and cast in molds she makes herself. An original clay model is made, and then a flexible rubber mold is poured. They are painted and dressed with as much care as she gives to her larger work.

The first miniature doll Sheila designed was a little wax baby in christening dress and blanket. Before she was even completed, the artist thought of the baby angel design, so the two ideas developed together. The baby in the blanket has no armature in her body which is cloth filled with polyester fiber. Her head, arms and legs are cast wax. The baby angel is the same construction, but she has a copper wire skeleton which enables her to sit up.

The doll house dolls were begun in 1979. They have cast wax heads and hands, composition lower legs, wire armatures and cloth bodies. Their hair is mohair which is individually dyed for each doll.

All Wallace dolls are done in limited editions. Most of them, in fact, are one-of-a-kind. They are only made fully dressed.

Sheila Wallace is a member of the United Federation of Doll Clubs (UFDC) and the Original Doll Artist Council of America (ODACA).

**Illustration 44-3.** 6in (15.2cm) *Baby in Christening Dress.* Head, arms and legs of cast wax. Cloth body filled with polyester fiber.

**Illustration 44-4.** 1" = 1' (2.5cm = 30.5cm) scale *Victorian Couple.* Cast wax heads, arms and legs. Flexible wire armature bodies. Hair of mohair.

**Illustration 44-5.** 1" = 1' (2.5cm = 30.5cm) scale *Victorian Man and Gay Nineties Man.* Cast wax heads, arms and legs. Flexible wire armature bodies. Hair of mohair.

**Illustration 44-6.** 1″ = 1′ (2.5cm = 30.5cm) scale *Gay Nineties Couple.* Cast wax heads, arms and legs. Flexible wire armature bodies. Hair of mohair.

**Illustration 44-7.** 6in (15.2cm) *Baby,* other dolls in proportion: *Marie Antoinette and Children.* Group of individually sculpted one-of-a-kind dolls. Modeled wax shoulder plates, lower limbs. Wire armature bodies. Inserted hair.

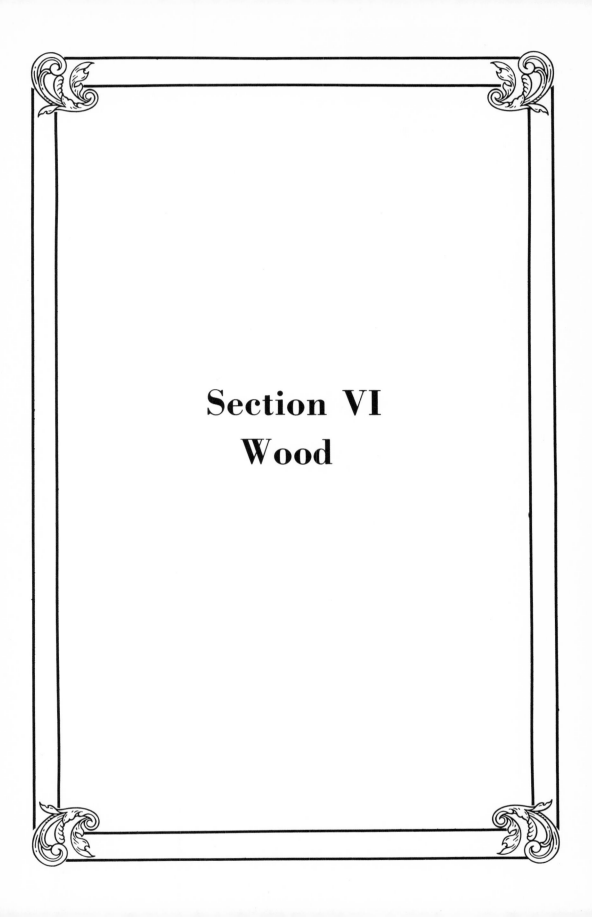

# Section VI
# Wood

Today's maker of wooden dolls bears little resemblance to Geppetto, the lovable old gentleman who fashioned *Pinocchio*. Yet their works sometimes seem to come to life even as his did.

Some of the first dolls to reach America were wooden ones - - the prim, stern-faced English Queen Anne dolls. These started an American love for jointed wooden dolls which is as much alive today as it ever was. Wood is such a native, available material. The whittling of a doll seems somehow an appropriate American pastime, producing an object evoking memories of American folk art and the cigar store Indian.

But it is not easy, as many a bandaged whittler's finger will attest. Wood carving is slow, laborious at times. Once a sliver is cut off, it is gone.

For a wooden doll to rise above the level of craftsmanship to any level of art, be it folk or fine, it has to be good. The miniature doll artists whose work follow carve their own versions of an American tradition in wood. They are the heirlooms of tomorrow.

# 45. Helena K. Beacham
## Wood

**Illustration 45-1.** Carved statuettes: *Little Girls*. Made before the artist began carving dolls.

Helena K. Beacham is a graduate of the Philadelphia College of Fine Art and studied sculpture with Beatrice Fenton. She paints and does ceramic figures and has been carving wood since the 1940s, making mainly small animals and delightfully awkward-stanced little girls. It was not until 1979, however, that she started making dolls.

At a doll show in the fall of that year, Mrs. Beacham came into contact with Helen McCook and her work. The inspiration and friendship which came of this encounter soon bore fruit. Since her carvings had such childlike, almost dolllike qualities already, Mrs. McCook encouraged Mrs. Beacham to push her work one step further, to create little articulated people. And she did.

Most of the Pennsylvania woman's dolls are small, less than 6in (15.2cm) tall, although occasionally they reach the height of 10in (25.4cm) or even 12in (30.5cm). They are completely wood, including the hair. The artist uses primarily basswood and dowels for her carving. Some of the smaller dolls are entirely made of dowels. Features and hair are painted.

The larger dolls are jointed at elbows and knees as well as hips and shoulders. The heads of some of the larger dolls can turn. This is accomplished by inserting a dowel into the basswood head which fits into a hole in the body. A pin in the back keeps it from making a complete turn.

Mrs. Beacham uses mostly hand-carving tools with short, round handles, chisels and gouges to fit each need and, of course, sandpaper. However, she does not try to disguise her medium, believing that carving should not "be lost" in the softness that sandpaper gives to wood.

Beacham dolls have a lovely innocence. They are plain and homely in the best sense of the word. Their creator says that she does not strive for fanciness in body or clothing.

Mrs. Beacham says she works as she has been told the Chinese wood carvers work. They say the spirit is in the wood, and they cut away and free it. She uses no models or photographs, but carves with just her memory to guide her. Sometimes when she is done her work reminds her of someone she knows.

Beacham dolls are one-of-a-kind. The artist completes approximately 16 dolls per year. She takes no orders, cannot duplicate her work and would not try. She simply enjoys

**Illustration 45-2.** 1" = 1' (2.5cm = 30.5cm) scale *Lady Godiva with Horse*. Carved wood. Painted features and hair. Jointed at arms and legs.

making little people and if someone else likes them, this pleases her. She sells her work through a small cooperative gallery near her home in Lahaska, Pennsylvania.

**Illustration 45-3.** 1″ = 1′ (2.5cm = 30.5cm) scale *Theresa, Elizabeth* and *Babies.* Carved wood bodies. Carved hair. Painted hair and features. Jointed at arms and legs.

**Illustration 45-5.** 1″ = 1′ (2.5cm = 30.5cm) scale *Adam, Mrs. Miniver, Tommy, Hetty* and *Babies.* Carved wood bodies. Carved hair. Painted hair and features. Jointed at arms and legs.

**Illustration 45-4.** 1″ = 1′ (2.5cm = 30.5cm) scale *Aunt Amanda* and *Patrick.* Carved wood bodies. Carved hair. Painted hair and features. Jointed at arms and legs.

**Illustration 45-6.** 10in (25.4cm) *Jenny* holding 1″ = 1′ (2.5cm = 30.5cm) scale *Doll House Girl.* Carved wood bodies. Carved hair. Painted hair and features. Jointed at arms and legs.

# 46. Patricia Ryan Brooks
# Wood, Polyform

**Illustration 46-1.** Patricia Ryan Brooks working on clay preliminary model for carved wooden portrait doll of Katharine Hepburn. 1979.

Nearly all of Patricia Ryan Brooks' dolls are portraits. Portraiture is a difficult specialty for any artist. It is especially challenging when the medium used is wood.

This is why the young Georgia artist produces two dolls for every one she sells. The first is a three-dimensional model in polyform (Super Sculpey). Here, photographs and sketches of the subject are used as a guide to capturing an exact likeness. The wooden doll is then carved, duplicating the modeled piece. In this way the NIADA artist is able to produce a doll that is so lively and fresh, it seems ready to speak.

Mrs. Brooks has been carving dolls since 1977. They have won armfuls of awards, including IDMA's (International Doll Makers Association) silver medallion, one of the most difficult prizes a doll maker can win. Despite her rapid advancement and great skill as a doll maker, she never considered doll making as a

career, but sort of fell into it. However, the basis for her sculpting talent is deep-seated.

Blessed with artistic parents, the Massachusetts native grew up in an aesthetic environment and absorbed its lessons by osmosis. She learned to look at the world with an artist's eye, a lesson which is seldom learned in art school. Later on, she sharpened her skills with formal college training. She had never, however, carved wood until November 1977, when she followed doll making instructions in an issue of *McCall's* magazine. It took her two long months to carve her initial effort because she had no one to teach her, and she was going to school full time.

**Illustration 46-2.** 5in (12.7cm) *Colleen, Pegeen* and *Gilligan.* Carved basswood. Articulated. Elastic strung. Carved-on shoes. Human hair. Carved horse and miniature rider. *Mrs. Alex Besyk Collection.* © 1980.

175

Illustration 46-3. 6in (15.2cm) *Punchinello.* Carved basswood. Wire armature body. Mohair wig. Produced in limited edition of six. © 1980.

Illustration 46-5. 8in (20.3cm) *Kendra.* Carved basswood. Articulated. Elastic strung. Mohair wig. Carved-on shoes. Carved horse and 3½in (8.9cm) miniature rider. *Mrs. W. Robert Whittaker Collection.* © 1979.

The carving fascinated her, and she persuaded an instructor to permit her to do doll carving for independent study. By the time her project was finished, Patricia knew that she had found her artistic niche.

In the spring of 1978, the young mother carved her second doll, her first miniature, a 4½in (11.5cm) portrait of her daughter, Katie. She dressed it after the outfit worn by Elizabeth Copley in the 1776 "Copley Family Portrait" by Boston artist, John Singleton Copley. Accompanying her were a 1¾in (4.5cm) wheeled horse and an extra tiny doll which sits atop the horse.

This trio won first place gold ribbon and best of class for miniatures (all media) and also the Jill Johnson Memorial Cup for overall best of show in the June 1978 IDMA doll show - - the first show Mrs. Brooks ever attended.

The doll show coup changed her life. Orders began pouring in and, although pregnant with her third daughter, she found herself a full-time doll artist with an ever-growing list of clients. The dolls seemed to sell themselves, even without advertising.

During the next two years the young artist continued to experiment with wood and to develop new sizes and subjects for her talents. She also began modeling dolls directly in polyform and working with vultex.

Brooks miniature dolls, 4in (10.2cm) to 8in (20.3cm), are fully carved from basswood. They are jointed at the shoulders and

Illustration 46-4. 8in (20.3cm) *Tyler* and *Teddy.* Carved basswood. Articulated. Elastic strung. Human hair. Carved bear. Portrait of Tyler Whittaker. *Mrs. W. Robert Whittaker Collection.* © 1980.

hips and have either human hair or mohair wigs. The 15in (38.1cm) to 20in (50.8cm) basswood dolls are peg-jointed at the shoulders, elbows, hips and knees with a mortise and tenon joint. They have additional swivel joints in the upper arms. Some have carved-on hair and also carved-on shoes. Others have human hair or mohair wigs and handmade removable shoes. All clothing is removable except on *Punchinello,* a new limited-edition *Commedia dell'arte* doll. The artist plans a series of these figures in editions of six each.

Except for the *Commedia dell'arte* figures and a 9in (25.4cm) cloth-bodied baby with wooden head and hands, all Brooks dolls (clay or wooden) are one-of-a-kind.

Mrs. Brooks credits her young daughter, Stephanie, with a "new look" in her work. Until that time, she states, most of her dolls were pouty types with little facial animation. She was working on the head of an 18in (45.7cm) portrait of her father's sister to be a companion to one she had done of him using a 1909 "pouty" photograph. Stephanie wandered in and watched her mother for a while and then

asked: "Mama, why don't you make happy dolls?" Mama put down her tools, took a critical look at her dolls and decided not to finish the one she had been working on. As she begins each new effort, Pat thinks of little Stephanie. Now, not only the facial expressions but the bodily attitudes as well of her creations transmit feelings of joy, wonder and excitement.

A steady stream of orders, workshops and doll making classes keep the NIADA artist busy. An understanding family has lent its support in many ways. The three Brooks daughters are the inspiration for many figures. They are helpfully impatient to see themselves "come alive." A supportive husband has lent his strength and photographic talent.

It is Pat Brooks' innate artistic skill though that has transformed inspiration into concrete form . . . or should we say wooden form?

Patricia Ryan Brooks is a member of the United Federation of Doll Clubs (UFDC) and the National Institute of American Doll Artists (NIADA).

**Illustration 46-6.** 8in (20.3cm) *La Danse.* Fully-carved and articulated 13-piece ball-jointed body. All sockets lined with kidskin. Polychromed. Jointed at neck, shoulders, elbows, waist, hips and knees. Old French lace tutu. © 1981.

**Illustration 46-7.** 9in (22.9cm) *Carrie O.* (Portrait of Caroline Olivia Brooks at age 2½ years.) Carved basswood. Wire armature. Human hair. Holding 1½in (3.8cm) *Doll.* Carved basswood head and body. Wire arms and legs. © 1981.

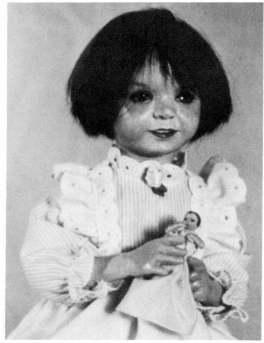

**Illustration 46-8.** Detail of Illustration 46-7.

**Illustration 46-9.** 1-7/8in (4.7cm) *Linden Bear* by Patricia Ryan Brooks. One-piece hand-carved one-of-a-kind teddy made of linden (bass) wood. Stained "fur," natural-color paws and snout. Black-painted eyes and nose, red-painted mouth. Green bow. Marked on bottom: Patricia Ryan Brooks N.I.A.D.A. 1981. Specially made for Carol-Lynn Waugh.

**Illustration 46-10.** 1-7/8in (4.7cm) *Linden Bear* by Patricia Ryan Brooks. Bottom view of Illustration 46-9, showing markings.

# 47. Judy Brown
# Wood

Judy Brown's wooden dolls are American folk art. To look at them brings back memories of limner paintings and 19th century folk sculpture.

These little people are 1/12th scale and are all wooden. Generally they are made of basswood, with hardwood joints, although some dolls are entirely carved of cherry, maple, birch, mahogany or walnut. The baby is jointed with wires at shoulders and hips, and the larger dolls have mortise and tenon joints with wooden peg fasteners at the shoulders, elbows, hips and knees.

**Illustration 47-2.** 5-1/3in (13.5cm) and 5¼in (13.4cm) *Wedding Cake Dolls.* Doll bodies basswood, legs and arms of light birch wood. Arm posts at shoulders attached to the backs of the dolls with small pegs. Hair carved on, painted with acrylics. Sealed with varnish.

The dolls' heads are stationary. Hair is carved in relief as a part of the head, especially in the lady dolls. Many men have the hair merely painted on. A few dolls have embroidery floss hair.

They are finished with a translucent mixture of varnish and artist's oil that lets the soft glow and warmth of the wood show through.

The Virginia doll maker has had no formal training in the arts but has always enjoyed a variety of craftwork, drawing, painting and sewing.

In 1975, she put them together, inspired by a doll-carving article in *McCall's Make it for Playtime, Dolls, Doll's Clothes and Toys.* Figuring that "anybody" must be able to copy a pattern printed in a magazine, she began experimenting. What she came up with

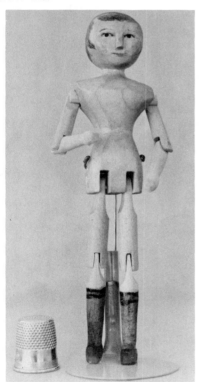

**Illustration 47-1.** 5-7/8in (14.9cm) *Man.* Doll body is basswood. Legs and arms are light birch wood. Arm posts at shoulders are attached to the back of the doll with small pegs. Hair painted on. Dark brown shoes and blue socks painted on. Finished with a mixture of varnish and artist's oils.

179

**Illustration 47-3.** 5½in (14.0cm) *Lady.* Body of basswood. Legs and arms of light birch wood. Arm posts at shoulders attached to the back of the doll with small pegs. Hair carved in relief. Small holes drilled in either side of face to hold glasses which are made of fine brass wire.

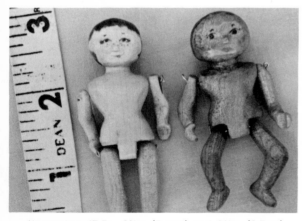

**Illustration 47-5.** 2¾in (7.1cm) and 2½in (6.7cm) *Babies.* Carved of two different shades of birch wood. Arms and legs joined to the body with fine wire. Dolls finished with varnish and artist's oils.

was pure Americana: tradition mixed with nostalgia.

Her dolls are abstract, depicting "ordinary people:" children, adults and babies. They range in size from 1½in (3.8cm) to 2½in (6.4cm) for babies, 2½in (6.4cm) to 3½in

**Illustration 47-4.** 5¾in (14.7cm) *Lady.* Body of basswood. Arms and legs of light birch wood. Arms attached at the shoulders with small brass screws. Face painted with acrylics, then varnished. Embroidery floss hair.

(8.9cm) for children and 5in (12.7cm) to 6in (15.2cm) for adults. They have no ears or fingers, and their slightly severe expressions mask their feelings. They are dressed generally in costumes from the late 1890s or early 1900s.

All clothing construction is done by hand, and Ms. Brown often uses old silk ties with tiny designs in them for the tiny garments, fitting the clothes to the dolls as she works.

This relatively modern dress on a traditional doll is somehow not incongruous. It is merely an updating of the old, sort of on the order of a contemporary updating of a 19th century quilting design. It works, as does all good folk art.

Judy Brown dolls are signed and year dated on their lower backs:

*Handcarved by Judy Brown Sterling, VA 1981*

in permanent ink.

Judy Brown serves on the Board of Directors of the North Virginia Handcrafters' Guild.

Illustration 47-6. 1¾in (4.5cm) *Doll House Dolly.* Birch wood. Arms are pegged to shoulder post. Both move at same time. Jointed at the hip and fastened with fine wire. Face, chest and hands painted with acrylics, then all varnished. Wears Mary Jane slippers. Embroidery floss braids.

Illustration 47-8. 6-1/8in (15.5cm) *Lady Doll.* Body carved of basswood. Limbs of light birch wood. Arm posts at shoulders are attached at the back of the doll with small pegs. Black shoes painted on. The heels of the shoes are carved as parts of the feet. Hair carved in relief.

Illustration 47-7. 6¼in (13.4cm) *Man.* Body carved of basswood. Limbs of light birch wood. Arm posts at shoulders are attached at the back of the doll with small pegs. Hair painted on. Shoes and socks painted on. Finished with a mixture of varnish and artist's oils.

Illustration 47-9. 5½in (14.0cm) *Lady Doll.* Body carved of basswood. Limbs of light birch wood. Arms attached at the shoulders with small brass screws, limiting arm action to backward and forward.

# 48. Patti Hale
# Wood

**Illustration 48-1.** Patti Hale at work.

Patti Hale's hand-carved dolls and bears are atypical. They seem ignorant of the fact that they are made of wood, so they refuse to conform to type.

They are neither stiff, flat, nor necessarily hard. Their rounded little cheeks and plump childish (or bearish) bodies look more like they were sculpted of clay than carved of wood. They are even put together in a clay-doll way. Their joints are not the Pinocchio-like mortise and tenon system but are, rather, like those of all-bisque dolls strung with elastic cord. Some are semi-articulated. Others are fully articulated with ball joints. Still others have carved heads and lower limbs on stuffed striped polyester fabric bodies which are wired for posing and for flexibility. The striped bodies are whence comes the nickname: "Peppermint Patti."

Patti Hale has been carving dolls since 1974. Although she has had extensive practical experience in many crafts, she is self-taught in the art of wood carving. Jelutong, wood from one of the rubber trees of Maylasia, is her preferred medium. It cuts very easily and has a nice, almost fleshlike appearance when finished with a sealer. She has also worked with pine, redwood and even avocado wood, the latter from trees on her property, but prefers the increasingly hard-to-find jelutong which has very little grain and few blemishes.

Her chief tool is a disposable-bladed X-Acto knife. "I do have carving tools but have never used them or even sharpened them," she says "Why change now? I'm doing just fine." She now uses a bandsaw to do dimensional cutting and save her fingers.

Peppermint Patti's dolls are in all sizes and types - - whatever comes into her head that she is able to transpose into wood. It is this transposing into wood that gives the dolls their charm, for their designer is not shackled as many wood-carvers are by "thinking wood" as she works. She "thinks doll" instead and transforms the wood to convey her thoughts.

She carves commissioned portraits, celebrity dolls and teddy bears, dolls representing all ages from babies (which she prefers) to the elderly. Even copies of old Kewpies or old composition dolls are within her ability.

The dolls range in height from several inches to about 21in (53.3cm). Miniature dolls are generally from 6in (15.2cm) to 8in (20.3cm) tall. Patti Hale does not make doll house dolls. She explains, "There is a size that is comfortable to carve, and the smaller and the larger becomes much more difficult, especially the doll house size. By the time you carve and file and sand, you lose detail."

These small creations are mostly "somewhat realistic" children, to use Patti Hale's term. She describes them as "cute, happy kids rather than 'people' figures. They are somewhat exaggerated and not strictly proportionate. As such, they are more pleasing to the eye."

Indeed they are. These articulated sculptures depict children from the early 1900s on up to contemporary time, *Mr.* and *Mrs. Santa Claus,* renderings of wedding portraits, ethnic dolls, elves, as well as carrousel and hobby horses. The latter are especially fine.

**Illustration 48-2.** 5in to 7in (12.7cm to 17.8cm) *Carrousel Kids.* Left to right: A and B: *Just Kids* (vary), *Miss Prim* (seated), *Valentine Krista* behind chair, *Colored Valentine Krista* with afro wig and *L'il Rufus.* Carved heads, hands and lower legs. Carved hair. Painted-on shoes. Poly striped, stuffed body. Wired.

And, not to be excluded, there are the teddy bears. These delightful, bemused critters are all wood and nearly always jointed. They sit and stand and are quite well behaved.

The California artist designs and makes all the clothing for her dolls. She sells them only fully dressed. "That's the fun part for me - - to make the complete doll - - the doll isn't done until it's dressed the way I want."

Freshness of expression and attention to detail are what set Hale dolls apart. Hands are generally gesticulating, with expressive fingers,

**Illustration 48-3.** 7½in (19.1cm) *Miss Prim* and 7in (17.8cm) *L'il Brother.* Carved wooden heads, hands and lower legs and shoes. Peppermint stripe polyester knit body. Poly stuffed. Wired for posing. Shown on hardwood base with velour covered and upholstered chair. Beaded and fringed electrically lighted lamp. © 1980. *Wanda Jackson Fernandez Collection.*

**Illustration 48-4.** 8in (20.3cm) *Eloise.* Artist's rendering from Kay Thompson's book. Carved wooden head, hands and lower legs and shoes. Peppermint stripe poly knit body. Poly stuffed and wired for posing. Hair wig. © 1980. *Edna Le Clerq Albrecht Collection.*

not the abstract spoon-like cups of more primitive dolls. And yet there is a gentle "folk arty" quality about these dolls. They seem to be in the same family with and very comfortable on the miniature carrousel horses.

In 1977, Patti Hale carved a *tour de force* carrousel, 22in (55.9cm) across, for the UFDC National Convention, held in San Diego, California, to complement its carrousel theme. This work was lighted and went round and round as the six horses (all different) moved up and down. Seven 6in (15.2cm) dolls (all different) sat on the horses and authentic carrousel music was provided by an organ box with a cassette tape in it.

Peppermint Patti has made hundreds of her little dolls. She does not do limited editions and does do multiples of the same doll, but each one is of necessity different because it is hand-done. Her work is found in the collections of many, many fanciers of artist dolls.

Patti Hale dolls are incised on the back of the neck:

date
NIADA
Patti Hale (or P. Hale)

All-wooden jointed dolls are sometimes marked on the back of the torso. The bears have "P.H." on the bottom of one foot and

Illustration 48-5. 2in to 4in (5.1cm to 12.7cm) *Teddy Bears.* Carved, all wooden. Larger bears are articulated. 1978-79. *Patti Hale Collection.*

Illustration 48-6. 4in (12.7cm) *Bear.* All wooden, articulated bear. Arms, legs, head move. Pink ribbon at neck. 1980.

"NIADA" on the bottom of the other. Dresses and/or coats have a cloth tag sewn in with

Patti Hale
NIADA.

Patti Hale is a member of the United Federation of Doll Clubs (UFDC) and the National Institute of American Doll Artists (NIADA).

Illustration 48-7. 7in (17.8cm) *Mr.* and *Mrs. Santa Claus.* Carved wooden heads, hands and lower legs/ shoes. Peppermint stripe poly knit body. Polyester stuffed. Wired for posing. Mohair wigs and bears. 1977. *Mildred Hirsch Collection.*

Illustration 48-8. 7in (17.8cm) *Brenda* and 7½in (19.1cm) *Bucky*. Carved wooden head, hands and lower legs and shoes. Peppermint stripe polyester knit body. Polyester stuffed. Wired for posing. Girl has curled mohair wig. Boy has carved hair. © 1980. *Madalaine Selfridge Collection.*

Illustration 48-9. 22in (55.9cm) across: *Carrousel.* Lighted. Goes round and round. Horses go up and down. Six horses, all different. Seven dolls, about 6in (15.2cm) tall, all different. All hand-carved. Organ box with cassette in it that plays authentic carrousel music.

Illustration 48-11. 5in to 7in (12.7cm to 17.8cm) *L'il Ruby* and *L'il Rufus, Jason on Flying Horse, Krista* in front, *Toby* in bonnet and *Krista* with wig (afro mohair). Carved wooden heads, hands and lower legs/shoes. Peppermint stripe polyester knit body stuffed with polyester fiberfill. Wired for posing.

Illustration 48-10. Detail of Illustration 48-9.

# 49. Connie Molak
# Wood

**Illustration 49-1.** 2in (5.1cm) *Boy with Teddy.* Carved pine. One-piece dolls. Oil painted clothes and features. Flat varnish finish.

Connie Molak carves wooden dolls of ponderosa or white pine wood using only an X-Acto knife with a No. 11 blade. Her dolls are of all sizes including miniature.

She started carving dolls in 1964 when her son was in the hospital for eye surgery. She brought along an X-Acto knife and a piece of wood to keep her busy while he slept. She made her first wooden doll in the hospital.

Since then she has made some 200 of them. Most of Connie's dolls have cloth bodies like those on antique dolls. A few of them are all wooden, jointed at the elbows, shoulders, hips and knees. She uses oil paint on the dolls' features and hair and a flat varnish overall.

She has depicted *Liza Minelli, Marilyn Monroe, Bilbo Baggins* from the book, *The Hobbit,* fairies, elves, Santas, children, flappers, *Abraham Lincoln,* teddy bears and rabbits. She has made portraits of people and miniature Queen Anne type dolls.

"I love to work with wood," she says. "It makes me happy. The wood is warm and friendly, and I forget my troubles. I am most happy when I am creating - - and I find that I am most responsive to people and therefore - - the dolls."

Connie Molak's dolls are signed on their legs and/or back.

Connie Molak is a member of the United Federation of Doll Clubs (UFDC).

**Illustration 49-2.** 1½in (3.8cm) *Boy with Teddy.* Carved pine. One-piece dolls. Oil painted clothes and features. Flat varnish finish.

**Illustration 49-3.** 6in (15.2cm) *Portrait of Abraham Lincoln.* Head, arms, legs and feet hand-carved of ponderosa pine. Cloth body made like an antique doll's body. Hair and features painted with oil paint. Flat varnish finish. One-of-a-kind original. *Private collection.*

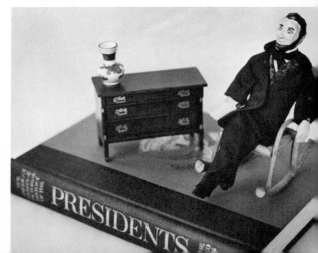

# 50. L. Duree Shiverick Wood

L. Duree Shiverick started life as a replacement for a doll. Her two older sisters had made up the name *Duree* for a cloth doll their mother had made before Duree herself was born. When she finally arrived, she took its place, name and all.

Since 1972, the Idaho native has been carving dolls. Her first doll was a Christmas gift for her niece, Wendy. As Duree had been carving other things for two years, it was natural to think of doll making in terms of wood for the gift. This first doll, 6¾in (17.2cm) tall, had a head carved from a spool, hands and feet from scraps of pine and a body of cloth. Her wig was human hair.

The wood-carver made several of the spool-headed dolls but when spools became scarce, she began using birch dowels. The body and head are now carved from one piece of wood. The dolls' limbs are jointed with tongue and groove joints at elbows, hips and knees and pinned through with fine wire. Woods are often mixed in the carving of a doll. Birch, maple and sometimes oak are most common for the arms and legs.

A talent for wood-carving runs in Ms. Shiverick's family. Her grandfather's, and uncle's fine craftsmanship in wood give her examples to emulate. She enjoys taking a rough piece of wood and a scrap of cloth and creating something which can arouse in someone else the same emotions she feels: wistfulness, gaiety, humor, and a sense of times gone by but not quite lost.

The dolls' hair almost always is made from human hair gleaned from friends, family or "unsuspecting youngsters with long hair." It is not uncommon for someone to order a doll for a child or adult and supply a hank of hair for its wig. Grey hair is particularly difficult to obtain, so it is the exception to the rule. This comes from full-size wigs which are taken apart and restyled for dolls. For either type of hair, the wigmaking method is the same. Lengths of at least 3in (7.6cm) to 4in (10.2cm) are required. A few strands at a time are glued onto the head until the basic hairstyle is completed. Then braided buns and ringlets are added. Ringlets are made by curling strands

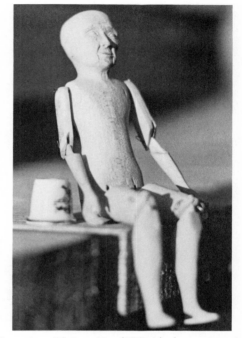

**Illustration 50-1.** 7in (17.8cm) (approximately) *Undressed Doll.* Hand-carved of birch. Tongue and groove joints at elbows, hips and knees. Pinned through with fine wire. Unpainted.

of hair on bamboo skewers. When the style is completed, it is sprayed several times with lacquer.

Ms. Shiverick designs and sews by hand all of her dolls' costumes and makes all of their accessories, with the exception of jewelry. She has dressed dolls in costumes from many periods but prefers the period circa 1880 to 1900.

"I suppose," she says, "this is because so many of my dolls are impressions of my great-aunts and grandmother, and I represent them doing the things they told me about when I was little and begged for stories about their childhoods (churning butter, beating eggs, sweeping and going to a church social)."

Only one costume has been repeated. Two dolls were made of a turn-of-the-century flower vendor.

**Illustration 50-3.** 7in (17.8cm) *Hazel, the Pedlar* and 7½in (21.6cm) *Liza, the Flower Vendor.* Completely carved from beech. Tongue and groove joints at elbows, hips and knees. Pinned through with fine wire. *Hazel* has grey hair from a nylon wig. Shawl of red wool. Dress and apron are cotton polyester. Tray of pine with a leather strap. Spoons carved from popsicle sticks, cookie jar from a spool, teapot from a mahogany dowel. Bowls and fruit from baker's clay and then enameled. *Liza* has human hair done in a braided bun in the back. Blouse of white polyester. Skirt of navy blue wool, shawl of cream-color wool. Hat and basket made of glue and string, painted with oil paint and trimmed with straw flowers.

**Illustration 50-2.** 6¾in (17.2cm) *Désirée.* First Shiverick doll carved with head and body in one piece. From a birch dowel. Arms and legs are also of birch. Tongue and groove joints at elbows, hips and knees pinned through with fine wire. Hair is human baby hair of Duree's sister for whom doll was made. Dress is of silky cream-color material, trimmed with cream-color lace and rust-color ribbon, gathered with silver beads.

It takes Ms. Shiverick about two full weeks to complete a doll.

The combinations of materials: the juxta-position of human hair with the wood, played against the softness of the garments which are made of a variety of materials, both synthetic and natural, make these dolls fascinating. The fact that they are, at times, recreations of ancestors and utilize real, known, people's hair gives a very personal dimension to their conception.

L. Duree Shiverick dolls are stamped on the back: "Hand carved by Duree." They bear a parchment tag reading the same.

**Illustration 50-4.** 7½in (21.6cm) *Greensleeves.* Hand-carved entirely of birch. Tongue and groove joints at elbows, hips and knees. Pinned through with fine wire. Human hair, painted features. Lute carved from pine, stained dark on the back. Dress of unbleached muslin. Overdress of brown polyester with velvet-like nap. Trimmed with braided embroidery thread.

**Illustration 50-5.** 7¼in (18.5cm) *Bill Dye* and 7in (17.8cm) *Emma, the Milkmaid. Bill Dye* is carved entirely of birch. *Emma's* head and body are birch. Legs and arms from pine. Tongue and groove joints at elbows, hips and knees. Pinned through with fine wire. *Bill's* long John shirt is a cotton knit with bead buttons. Blue denim overalls. Bamboo hoe-handle. Copper blade. *Emma* has human baby hair. Dress of yellow cotton. Overskirt of gold cotton polyester. Jerkin of blue leather laced with yellow thread. Yoke she bears is carved from pine, the buckets from spools.

**Illustration 50-6.** 7in (17.8cm) *José* and 6¾in (17.2cm) *Felipa.* Basque dancers. Carved from birch with maple legs and arms. Tongue and groove joints at elbows, hips and knees. Pinned through with fine wire. Human hair. *José's* shirt and pants of white cotton, sash of red cotton. Hat of red felt. "Bells" at knees are brass beads sewn onto imitation leather. Shoes of both dolls are felt and glue, painted black. *Felipa's* blouse and scarf of white cotton, skirt of red cotton. Vest and apron of black cotton.

**Illustration 50-7.** 8½in (21.6cm) *Mattie* and 7¼in (18.5cm) *Teres.* Both hand-carved of birch. Tongue and groove joints at elbow, hip and knee. Pinned through with fine wire. Human hair. *Mattie* dressed in burgundy velvet dress trimmed with black crepe. White crepe blouse overlaid with lace. Brass bead buttons. Burgundy velvet hat stiffened with wire, trimmed with gilded lace, black ostrich feathers and yellow flowers. Back of hair done in ringlets. *Teres'* bonnet is brown velveteen lined with yellow cotton. Blouse is yellow polyester trimmed with yellow satin ribbon. Dress is yellow polyester trimmed with white lace, yellow satin ribbon and yellow beads. Shawl of cotton lace.

**Illustration 50-8.** 7in (17.8cm) *Charlotte* and 8in (20.3cm) *Scarlet. Charlotte* is hand-carved from birch. *Scarlet* has head carved from a spool. Body is pine as are her arms and legs. Both have human hair. *Charlotte's* dress is of a white and brown cotton print. Skirt has a draped over-skirt with a bustle in the back. Blouse has mutton leg sleeves, white bead buttons, a rounded unbleached muslin collar. Poke bonnet is string and glue painted with oil paint and lined with unbleached muslin. It is trimmed with yellow straw flowers and tied with yellow satin ribbon. *Scarlet's* apron and bonnet are of unbleached muslin. Bonnet trimmed with beige nylon lace. Blouse of rust-colored polyester. Skirt of a coarse weave polyester. *Sandy Lavoie Collection.*

189

# Glossary

ARMATURE. In sculpture, an armature is a sturdy structure, usually made of metal and/or wood, which supports the material of which the sculpture is made. When a sculpture is made of a heavy material and is particularly large, there is danger that, unsupported, it could collapse from sheer weight.

A wire armature for a doll can be formed of twisted wires in the general shape of the doll body. This acts as a poseable skeleton upon which the rest of the body can be built up, of fabric or clay or other material.

ARTISAN. An artisan is a craftsman who is an expert in performing a particular skill.

BISQUE. Fired, unglazed clay. Any natural clay can be bisque; stoneware, terra cotta, and porcelain are among them.

BREAD DOUGH. A sculpting medium formed by adding various ingredients to squished-up slices of bread, and then kneading it. Among the ingredients added may be glycerine, white glue or acrylic paint. This mixture has a clay-like texture and can be modeled. It dries out quickly.

CASTING. This word can be either a noun or a verb. Casting (verb) is the act of pouring a substance (clay, wax, metal, etc.) into a mold to make a copy of a sculpted piece. A casting is the product that results from this procedure. SLIP-CASTING is the pouring of "slip" (usually liquid clay) into a mold.

CERAMIC. Referring to clay. All clays are ceramic. However, there is a popularly used clay that is purveyed by "ceramic" shops which is greyish in color before firing. When fired, it is a chalky white. It fires at cone 05. It cannot be china painted. Many people, when speaking of "ceramics," mean only this clay, which is usually slip-cast.

CHINA. Clay that has been fired and glazed. It has a glassy, shiny look, like that of china dishes.

CHINA PAINT. (Also called OVERGLAZE). The traditional way to decorate porcelain dolls is with overglazes (china paints). These pigments must be ground on a glass slab with small amounts of special overglaze flux. Oils are used as vehicles for painting, among them lavender oil, fat oil of turpentine and oil of balsam. After drying, the china painted article is placed into the kiln and fired to a relatively low, well-regulated temperature, so the pigments will melt and fuse to the clay, but not evaporate. Several firings are usually necessary in the decoration of a doll.

CLAY. Natural clay is of many types and textures. It can be fired in a kiln at various temperatures, depending upon the clay body's makeup. It is an excellent sculpting material, if care is taken to prevent it from drying too rapidly. Synthetic clay is a mixture of, usually, natural and man-made materials. Some synthetic clays can be baked hard in kitchen ovens. Others air dry. Still others cannot be fired at all and are used solely for sculpting purposes. A mold must be made from them if a permanent sculpture is desired.

COMPOSITION. In doll making, composition is traditionally a mixture of various substances which will form a modeling compound. The basis of composition often is sawdust. It is mixed with glue, plaster and other materials, depending upon the person making the composition. A "composition" in artistic terms means the arrangement of parts in an art object. For example: the composition of a painting, or of a sculpture.

CONE. A cone is an instrument for measuring temperatures in a kiln. Made of clay, it is shaped like a long, thin pyramid. A number stamped into its side identifies its melting point. It is placed in the kiln to indicate its interior temperature, when viewed from a peephole in the side of the kiln. When it begins to bend, the kiln can be turned off. Some electric kilns have automatic "kiln sitters," into which a cone is placed. When it bends, the kiln sitter turns the kiln off.

PYROMETRIC CONES have been so reliable that ceramists commonly refer to firing temperatures in terms of cone number. Cones are numbered up and down the scale from 022 through 01 and 1 up to cone 15. Cone 022 is 1121F (605 centigrade). Cone 15 is 2615F (1435C). Overglaze colors (china paints) mature at 019 (1220F) or 018 (1328F). "Low-fire" clays (like "ceramic" slip or terra cotta) mature at 06 (1859F). Slipcast porcelain usually matures at cone 5 (2201F) or cone 6 (2246F). Stoneware clays mature at cone 9 (2345F). High-fire porcelain matures about cone 13 (2462F), although some matures at cone 10 (2381F) or 11 (2417F), along with other white clays.

COPYRIGHT. The exclusive right, guaranteed by law, usually to an author or artist, for the publication, production or sale of the rights to a literary, musical, dramatic or artistic work. These rights are granted for a designated period of time, depending on the country in which they are granted.

DIRECTLY SCULPTED. A direct sculpture uses no molds for its final product. The sculpting directly into the final clay, wax or wood from which the doll will be made ensures that the directly sculpted doll will be one-of-a-kind.

However, a mold MAY be made of a directly sculpted doll, for editions to be made of it in some other medium.

DOLL ARTISAN GUILD. An organization formed in Oneonta, New York, for the popularizing and the preservation of the techniques of making reproduction dolls of porcelain.

DOLL ARTIST. A doll artist designs original dolls. These may be made of any sculptural medium, from cloth to clay. Often, but not always, a doll artist executes his own designs in permanent materials, which may be different from those in which the original design was sculpted.

EDITION. An ARTIST'S EDITION is a predetermined number of duplicates of an art object and is made by the artist himself. A LIMITED EDITION means that there is a finite number of objects in an edition. A CLOSED EDITION is one that is no longer being made.

FETTLE. To trim edges off, as with clay.

FIMO. A pre-colored, imported German synthetic clay that can be hardened at low temperatures in a kitchen oven. Colors can be intermixed to obtain many shades.

FIRE. Clay is hardened by fire. In ceramic terms, this word, when used as a verb, means "to cook." This is usually done in a kiln, using high heat.

GLAZE. A suspension of clay and mineral ingredients (in powdered form) in water. This mixture is painted onto a kiln-fireable clay, either before or after firing, depending upon the clay body used. Actually, "glaze" is a form of glass. It is an ancient method of making clay more durable and water resistant. It also makes it attractive. A glaze may be shiny (glossy) or not (matte).

GOOD BEARS OF THE WORLD. An international non-profit, tax exempt organization chartered in 1973 in Bern, Switzerland, believing in love and friendship, with understanding. One of the primary goals of the Good Bears of the World is to provide teddy bears as comfort for children of all ages in hospitals, institutions and generally everywhere. This organization may be contacted at: Good Bears of the World, P.O. Box 8236, Honolulu, Hawaii, USA, 96815, Telephone: (808) 946-2844.

IDMA International Doll Makers Association. Formed in Texas under the aegis of the late Jill Johnson, this organization welcomes all doll makers and is dedicated to the promoting of doll making worldwide. It holds annual conventions at which doll makers compete and learn new techniques.

KILN. A chamber for firing ceramic materials. It may be gas or electric powered, indoor or outdoor, small or large, depending on the needs of the ceramist.

LATEX. Rubber. It usually comes in a liquid state for artistic purposes. Combined with clay, water and chemicals, it forms "composition slip," which may be poured into molds for making editions of sculptures. Latex may also be used for making molds of sculptures.

LEATHER HARD. In clay: a degree of hardness in which the clay is neither extremely wet, nor bone dry. Enough moisture has evaporated from it for it to be easily handled. At this stage, in sculpture, clay edges can be joined together successfully.

MASTER SCULPTURE. A sculpture from which molds may be taken for the making of duplicates. This sculpture may be the primary sculpture of the artist, but a primary sculpture is often made of materials which are unsuitable for molds to be made repeatedly from it. Often, a master sculpture is cast in a permanent material into a mold made of a primary sculpture. The master sculpture is then cleaned and smoothed to make it suitable for molds to be made from IT.

MEDIUM. Any material used for expression in art. Plural: mediums, media.

MINIATURE. Smaller than life-size. A common scale for sizing miniatures in the United States is 1:12. That is, the object is 1/12 life size. Another way of expressing this is one inch equals one foot (1" = 1' [2.5cm = 30.5cm]). Other popular scales are 1/2" = 1' (1.3cm = 30.5cm), 3/4" = 1' (2.0cm = 30.5cm) and 2" = 1' (5.1cm = 30.5cm). The United Federation of Doll Clubs considers dolls to be miniatures if they're under 9in (22.9cm) in height.

MINI TONGA SOCIETY. A society of miniaturists who admire Sir Arthur Conan Doyle's fictional detective, Sherlock Holmes. They recreate scenes from the stories using miniatures. Tonga was the smallest character to appear in the Sherlock Holmes mysteries (referred to as THE CANON by followers). He appeared in the story "The Speckled Band."

MODELED. Modeled clay is clay which is worked with the hands. Dabs of clay are added and subtracted (sometimes with the aid of a sculpting tool) in the process of making a sculpture.

MOHAIR. The hair of the angora goat, long used for wigs for dolls and usually sold in hanks resembling one large fat curl. This fine-textured hair can readily be curled and styled and is in good scale for miniature dolls' hair.

MOLDS. For the reproduction of a sculpture, a mold is necessary. There are several substances which will serve for mold making, depending on the material of which the sculpture will finally be cast. A type of latex can be brushed on in successive coats to form a highly detailed flexible mold. This should be encased in a plaster outer shell. Latex, or rubberized molds cannot be used in slip-casting for porcelain or latex composition. A mold which will absorb the water content of the slip is necessary. Casting plaster or dental plaster is usually used for these molds.

REDUCTION MOLDS. A reduction mold is made from a piece of fired porcelain or other clay. In firing, the clay has shrunken somewhat from its original size. If a mold is made from this piece and then another piece of porcelain is cast in the mold made from the first item, and then fired, the resulting piece of porcelain will be reduced in size. If a whole series of molds of this sort is made, a doll can be fabricated in any number of sizes.

MONOCHROMATIC. Having a single color. A monochromatic painting is done in a single color or in varying shades of the same color.

MULTIPLES. In doll making, this term is usually applied to artists' work of which more than one of a kind is made.

NAME National Association of Miniature Enthusiasts. This organization has local chapters of amateur and professional miniaturists who promote the making, displaying and preservation of miniatures. They hold annual national and regional conventions at which workshops are held and craftsmen who work in miniature scale purvey their wares.

NEEDLESCULPTURE. A technique of modeling fabric by use of needle and thread. Often, nylon stocking is used as a base for this work.

NIADA The National Institute of American Doll Artists. The first and most exclusive of American doll artist associations. It promotes the doll as an art form. All of its members have the highest artistic standards for their work. Membership is highly selective, by invitation only.

ODACA Original Doll Artist Council of America. Formed in 1976 by doll artist Bess Fantl, ODACA is an association of working doll artists who have banded together for several reasons. One is professional cross stimulation. Another is mutual aid. A third is to guarantee the high standards and quality of their work to the buying public. Membership is selective, by invitation only.

ONE-OF-A-KIND. Some media demand that a doll made in them be one-of-a-kind. This means that no other doll is exactly like it, even though there may be similar ones executed by the same artist. Cloth, wood and directly-sculpted clay and wax are among these media.

OVERGLAZE. See china painting.

ORIGINAL. This term is often misused. An original doll is one that is *wholly* the conception and execution of the artist making it, from the first blob of clay to the last stitch on its dress. It can never be an adaptation of anyone else's work. An original doll *cannot* be one that is poured from a purchased mold and perhaps altered in the greenware stage, or a reproduction painted in a different "original" manner from the way this doll is usually done. It cannot be one which starts, perhaps, with an antique doll head from which a mold is made by a doll maker, who then pours porcelain into it and adds new corkscrew curls to the casting at the wet clay stage. There is no such bird as an "original reproduction." These two words are mutually exclusive. An original doll derives in no way from the work of another, living or dead.

PAPIER-MÂCHÉ. In French, these words mean "chewed paper." This substance is usually made of bits of shredded paper, water and glue which are mixed together to form a modeling compound. When dry, it can be sanded and painted.

PLASTER. In doll making this substance has several uses. Dental or casting plaster is used for molds. It is used in small quantities for setting in glass doll eyes. It is at times poured into wax castings to give them more durability. Master castings of sculptures are often done in plaster. Some doll parts are even cast in plaster.

PLASTICENE OR PLASTILINA. This clay is a mixture of natural clay, petroleum and other substances. It is a bit greasy, usually is a greyish color and it does not dry out. It is available in several hardnesses. It is excellent for sculpting as it responds readily (sometimes too readily) to the slightest touch. A mold must be made of a plasticene sculpture, as it is extremely malleable.

POLYCHROME. This term means to paint in several colors.

POLYFORM. This is the name of the company that manufactures the synthetic clays called SCULPEY and SUPER SCULPEY. These clays are a bit rubbery in texture. They are clean and can be easily baked in a home oven, sanded, added to and rebaked. The clays are often referred to by the company name, polyform.

PORCELAIN. A very fine-grained delicate clay which fires at a high temperature. It has a refined texture and is usually non-porous in the fired state. It is difficult to work with. Modern porcelain slip (liquid porcelain clay) fires at a lower temperature than solid porcelain clay. Early porcelain dolls were pressed into molds and made of the higher-firing clay. Today's porcelain is more durable than the old, thanks to modern chemistry. Porcelain has only been readily available to the home ceramist in America since the 1950s. Its development is really an offshoot of the American space program's search for durable, heat-resistant materials for use in rockets.

REPRODUCTION. A reproduction is a copy of an object made by another person. A reproduction doll is one made by a person other than the person who designed it, even if the reproduction artisan uses the original artist's molds. All reproductions should be signed and dated in a permanent manner (incision is best).

SCULPEY, SUPER SCULPEY. See Polyform.

SHOULDER PLATE. On dolls, this refers to a section of the doll containing, usually, the head, neck and shoulders. Sometimes the shoulder plate contains part of the torso or breast of the doll. There are usually holes in the shoulder plate for attaching it onto the doll's body.

SLIP. Clay to which water has been added so that it can be poured into a mold. It usually has the consistency of cream or of a milk shake. By extension, the term is used for other similar substances which can be poured into molds.

STONEWARE. A type of clay that matures at lower temperatures than porcelain, usually between cone four and cone eight. Stoneware is rarely white, usually fires some shade of brown or gray. It has a rougher texture than porcelain and is suitable for large sculptures.

TERRA-COTTA. Usually firing some shade of red, although it may also be buff or grey, this clay matures between cone 06 and cone 04 and is well suited to ceramic sculpture.

UFDC United Federation of Doll Clubs. This organization promotes the collecting of, and knowledge about, antique dolls. Its United States membership is divided up into regions of doll clubs (there are some members-at-large). They stage doll conventions. An annual national convention is held at which workshops, meetings, competitions and exhibits of dolls - - both antique and modern - - are the highlights.

WAX. Wax is an age-old medium for sculpture and doll making. It can be worked in many different ways: modeling, carving and casting, among them.

WAX-OVER. This doll making process consists of dipping a doll head made of some other material (clay, composition, papier-mâché, porcelain, etc.) into wax and then removing it. This procedure is repeated as often as the doll maker needs to do so. Thus, a wax-over doll may have any thickness of wax on top of its "core."

# INDEX

198